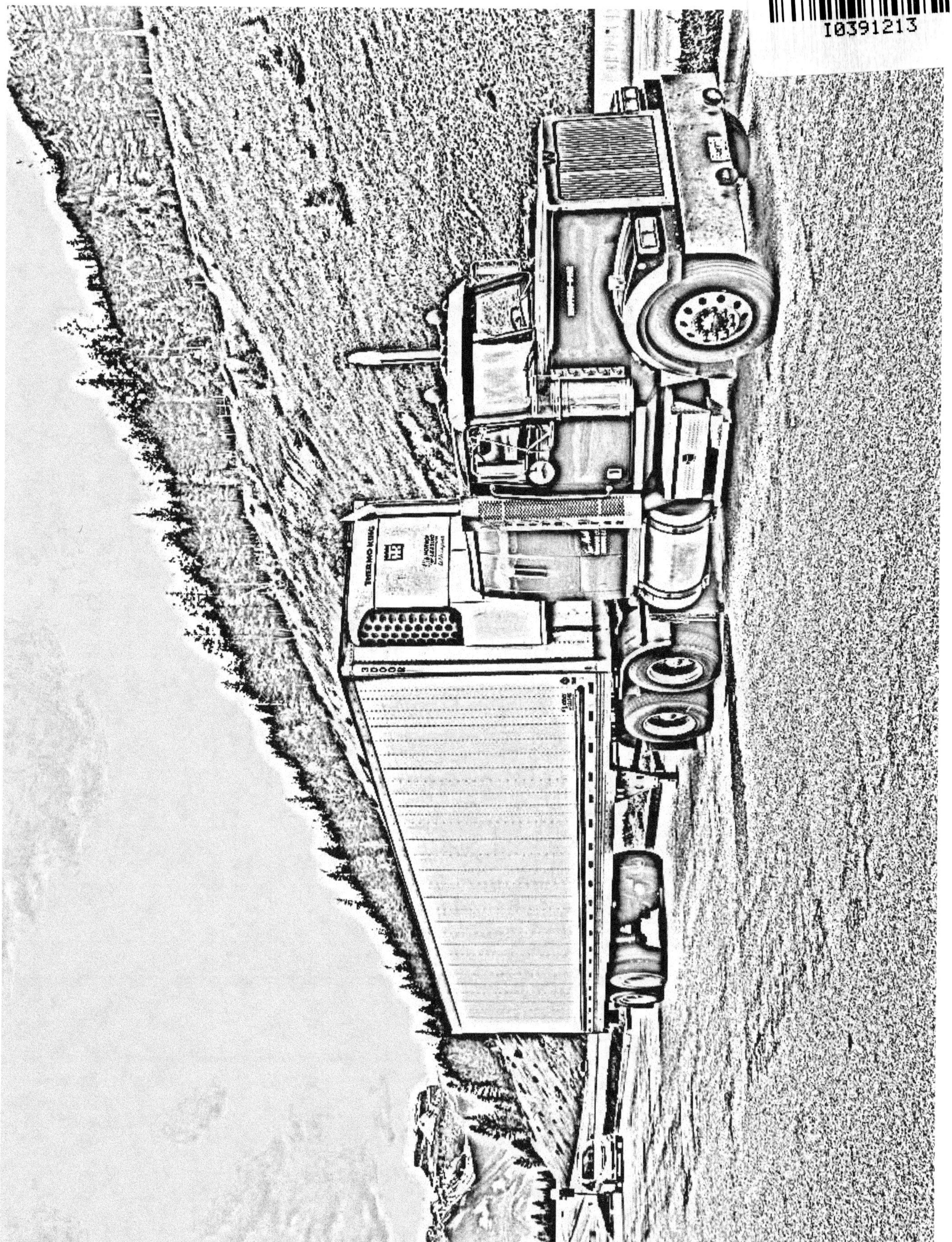

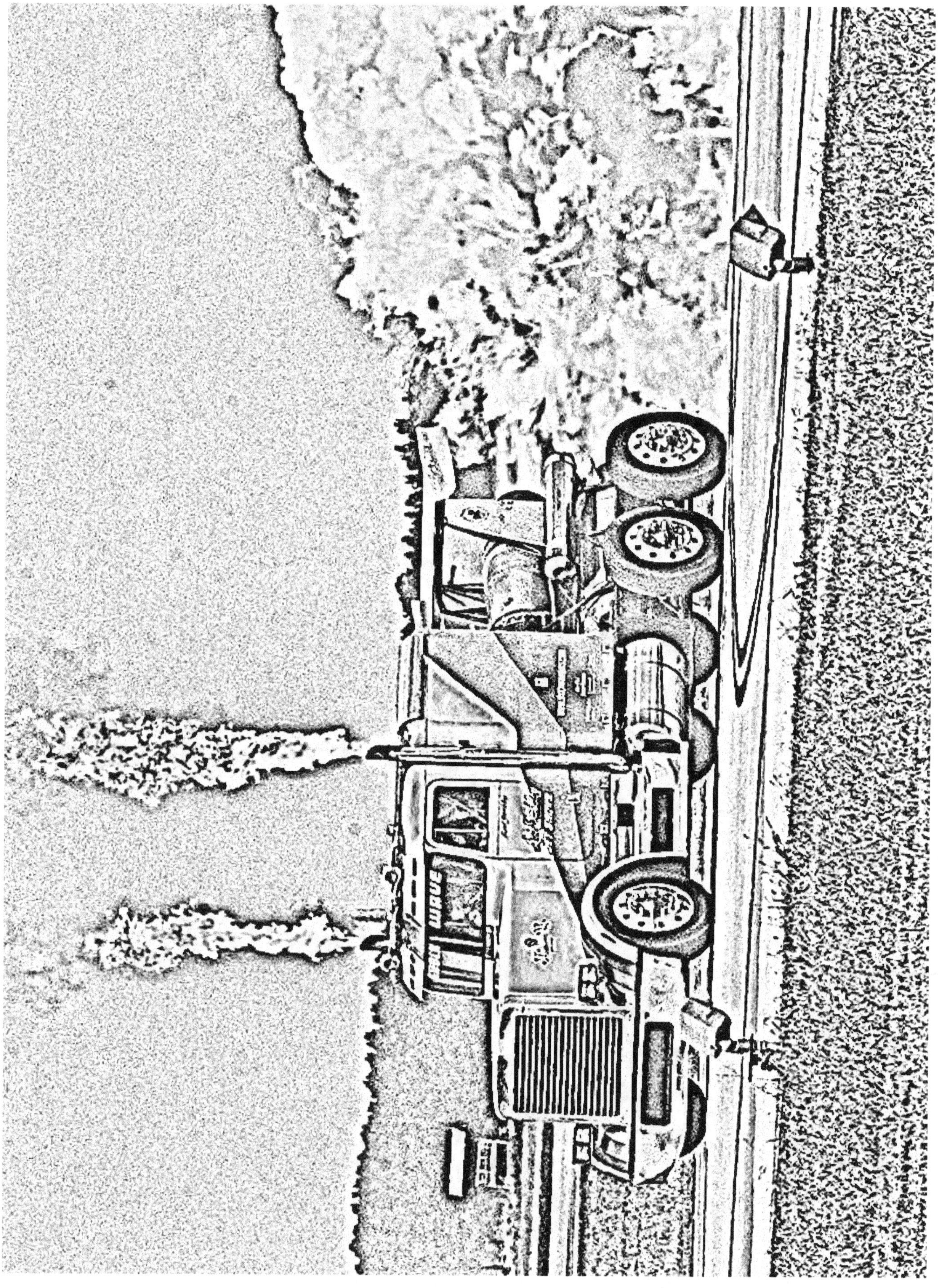

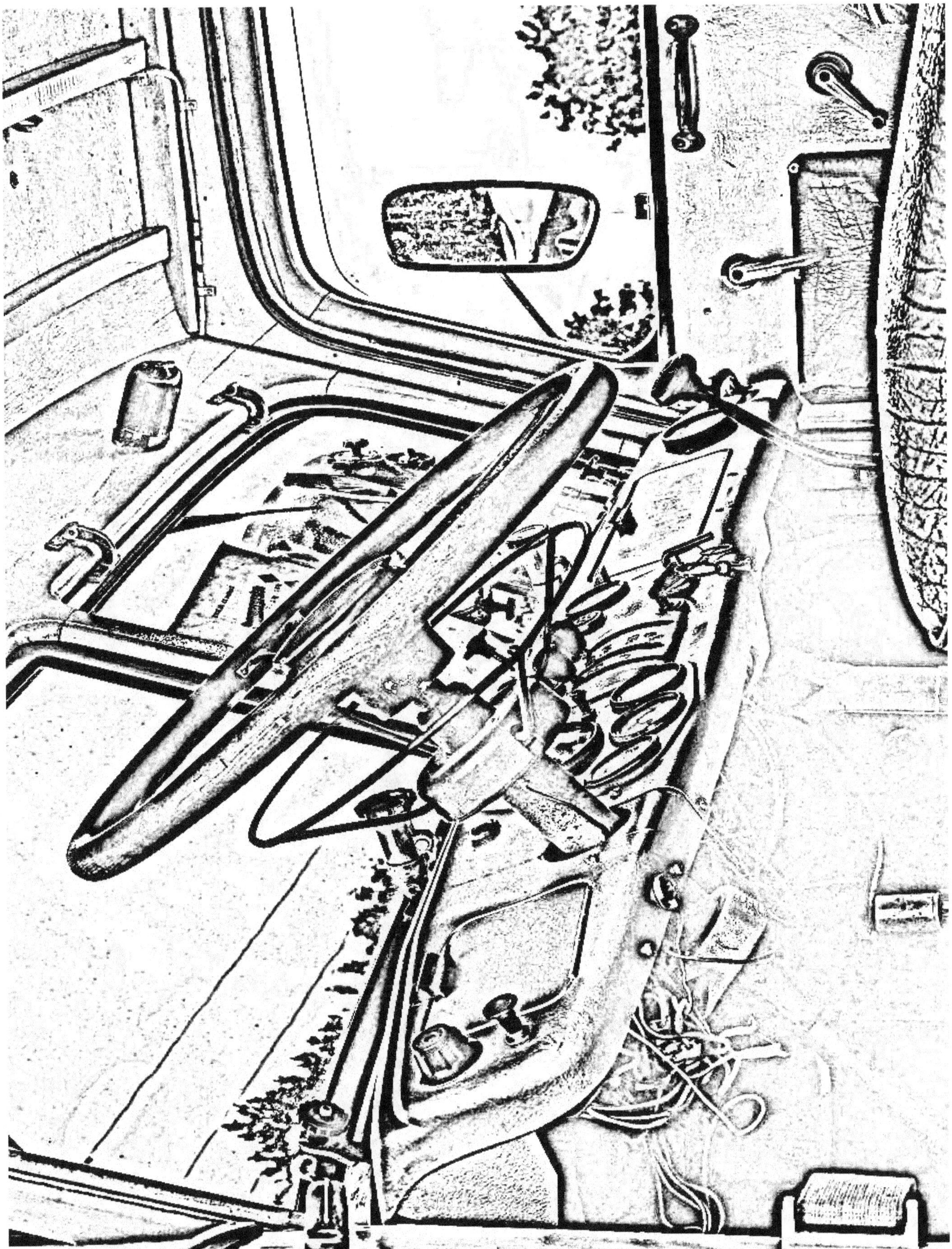

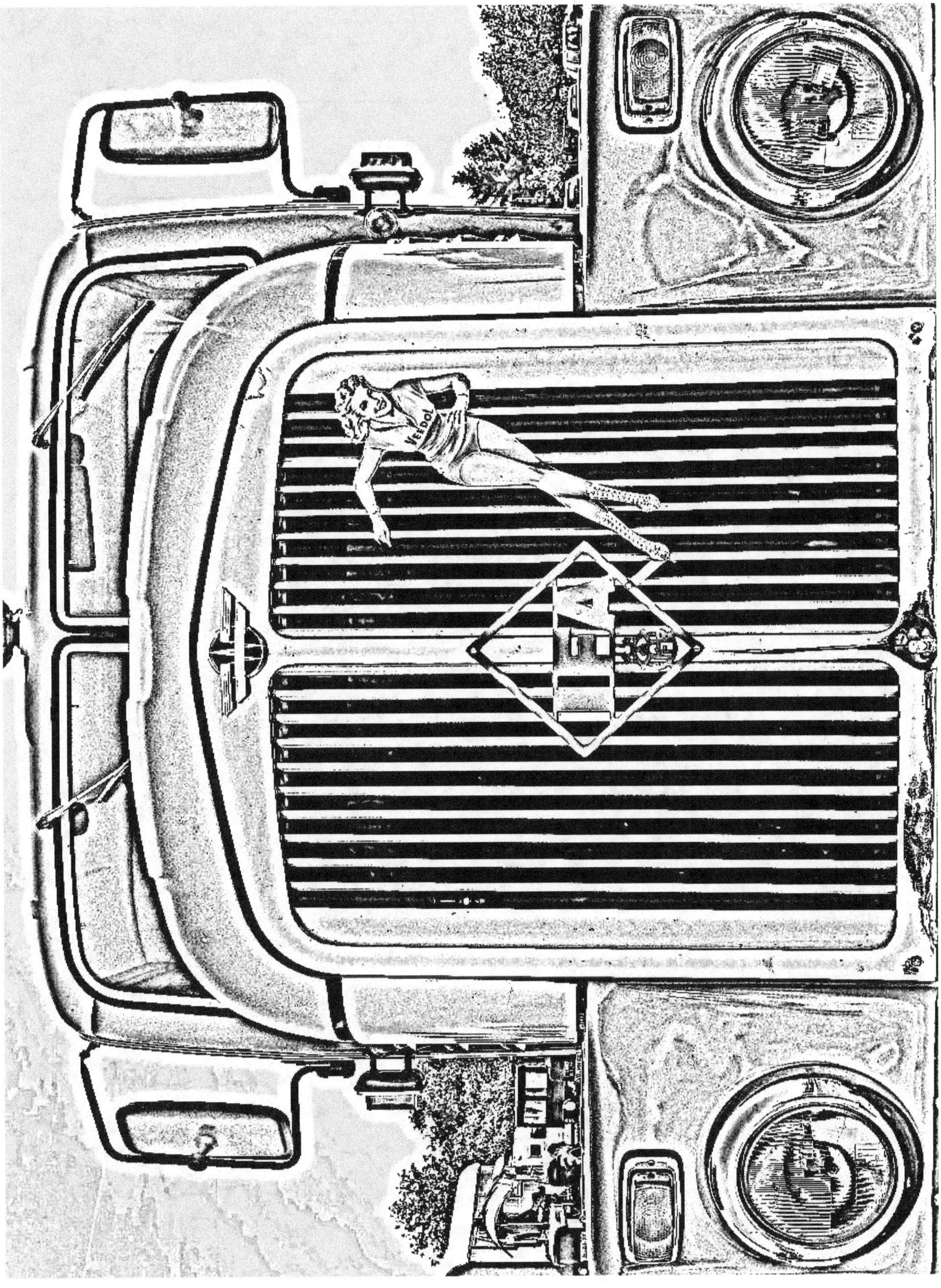

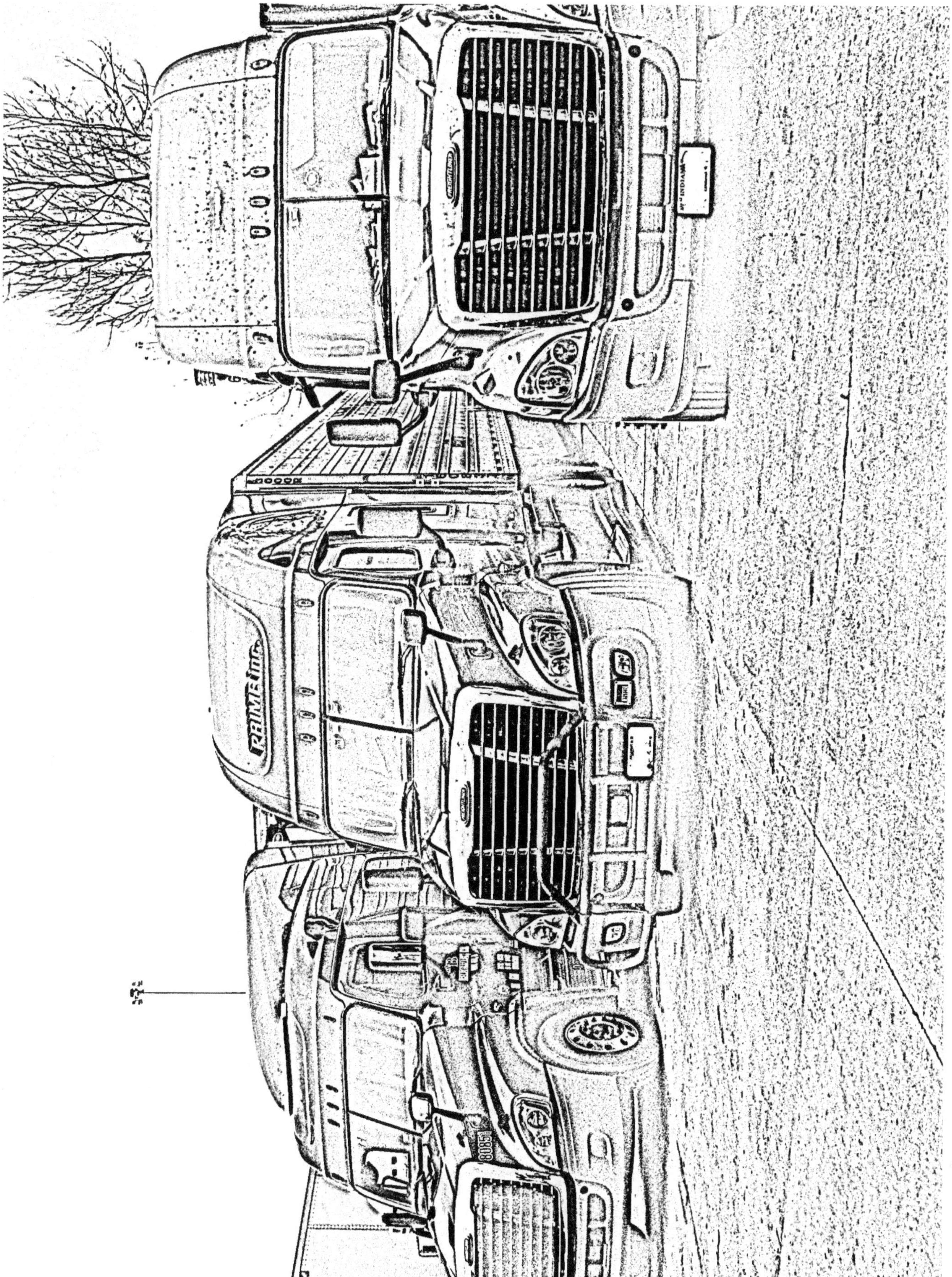
PRIME Inc.

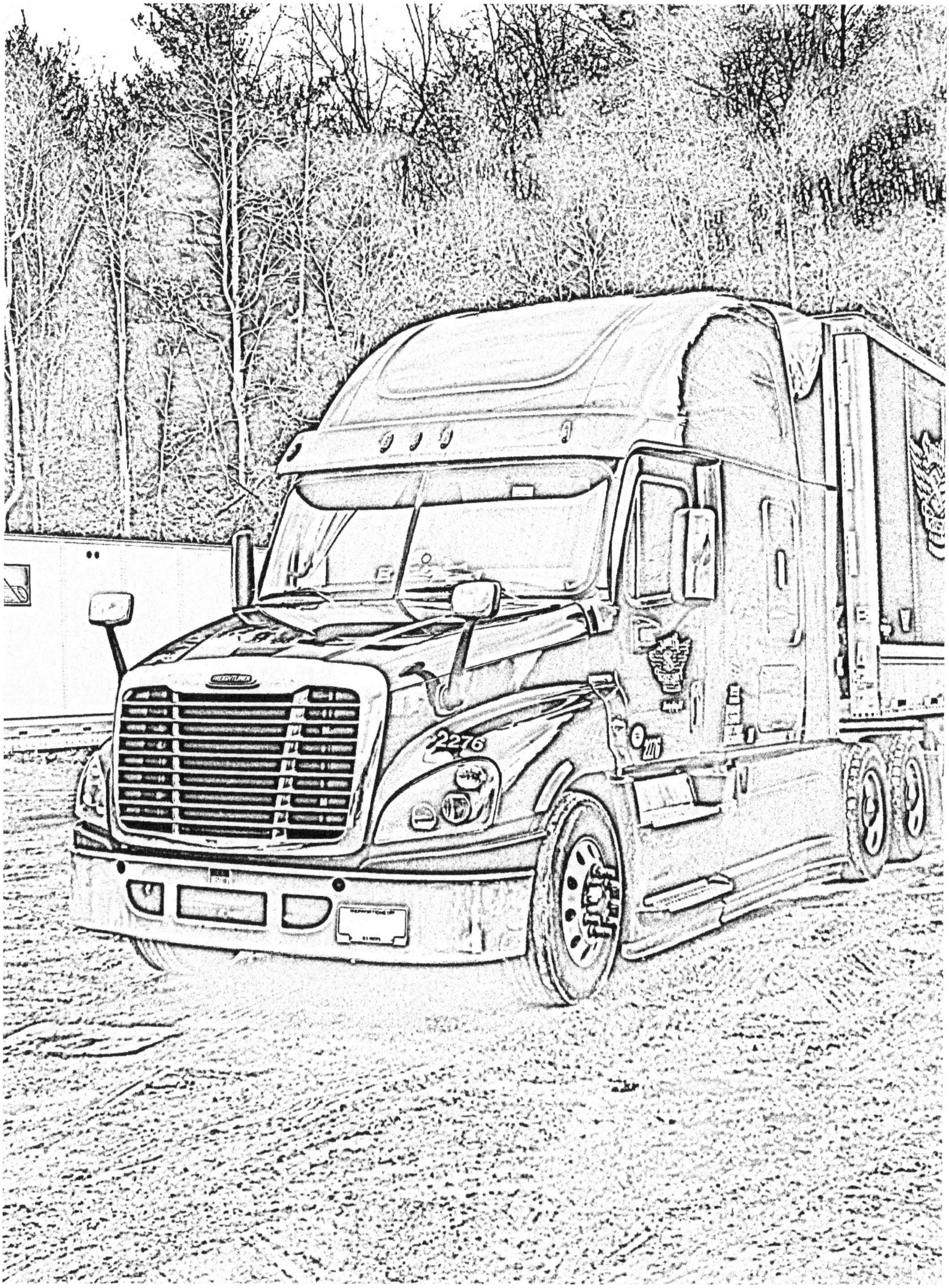
2276

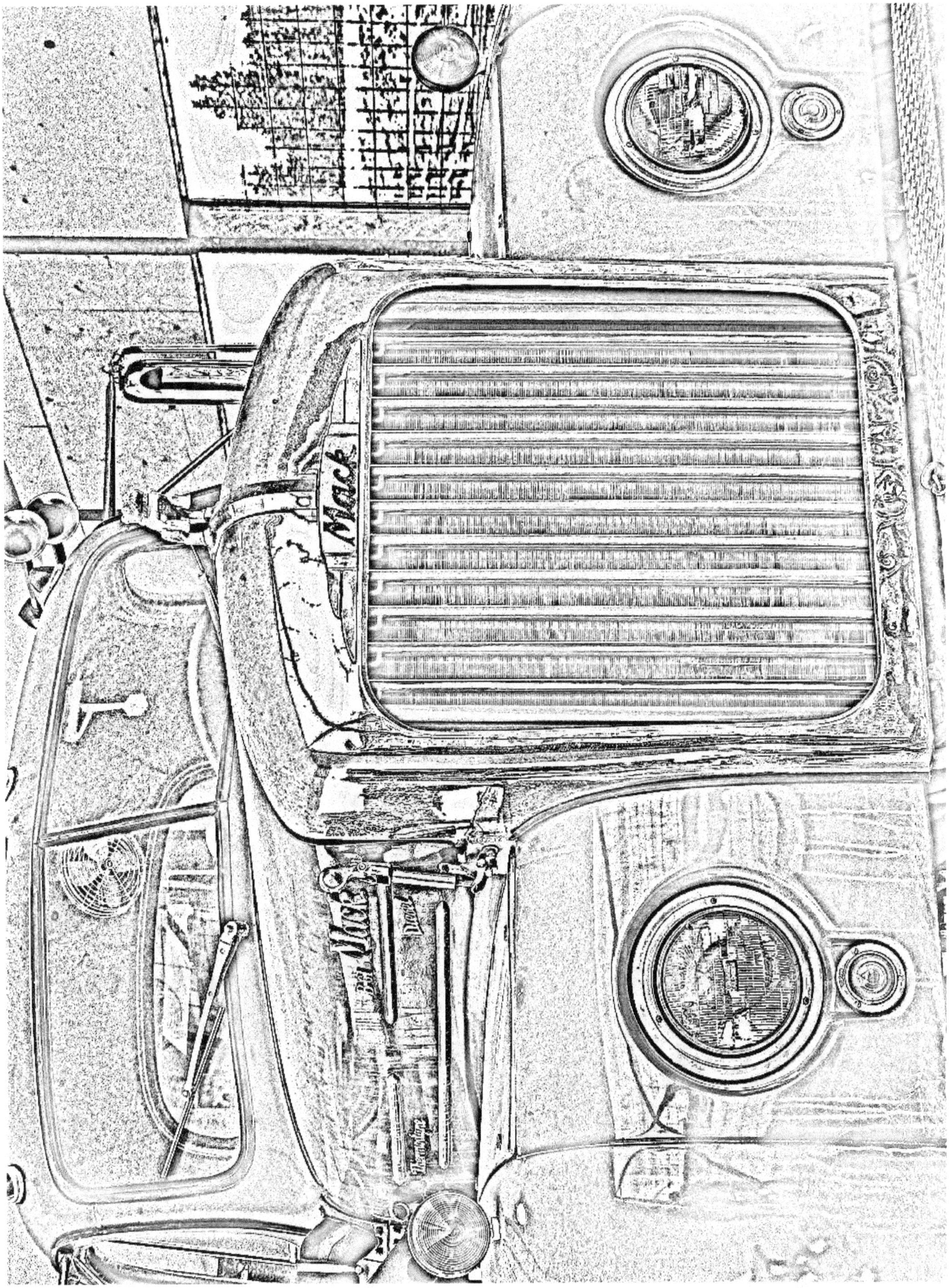
Mack

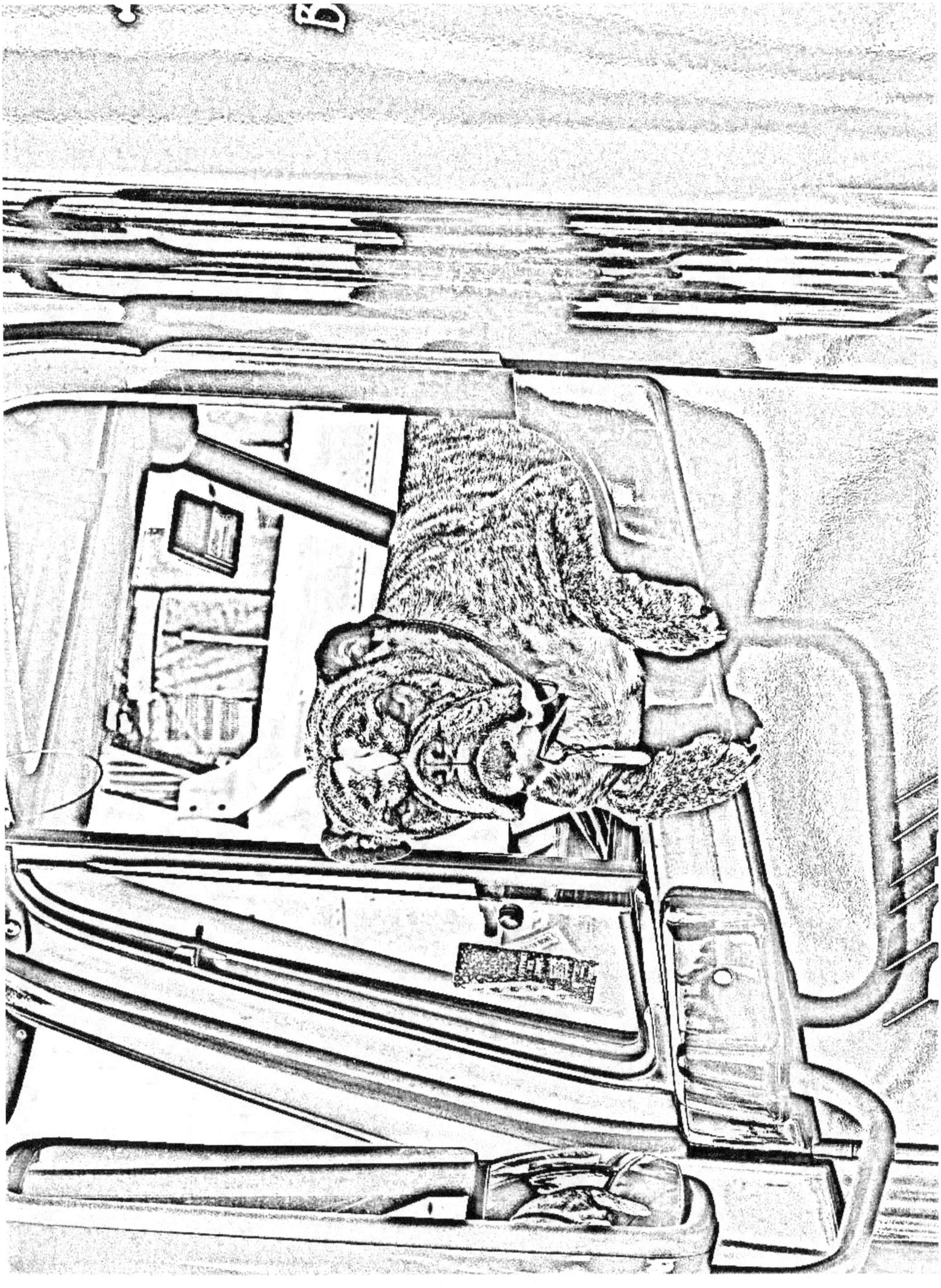

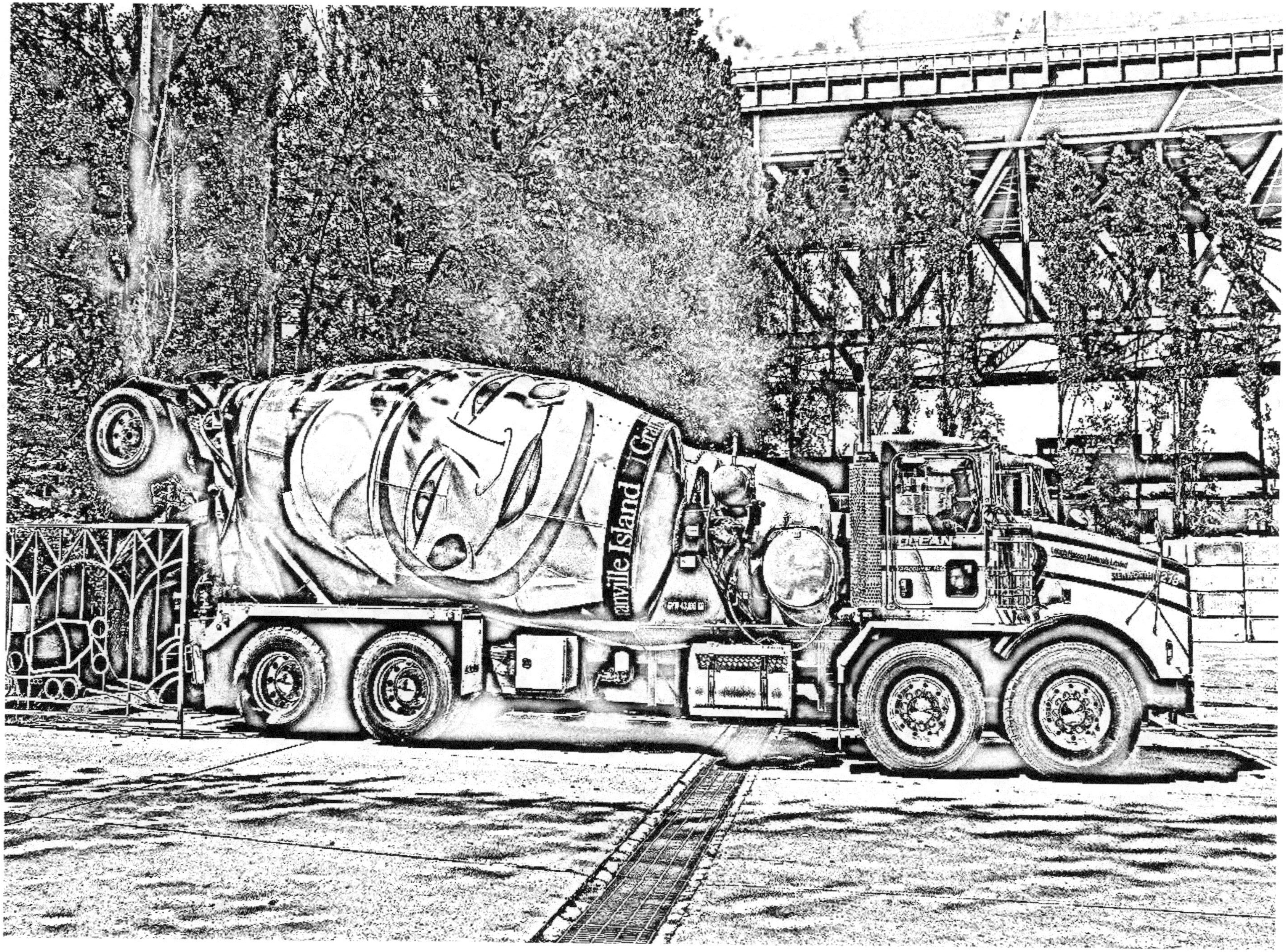

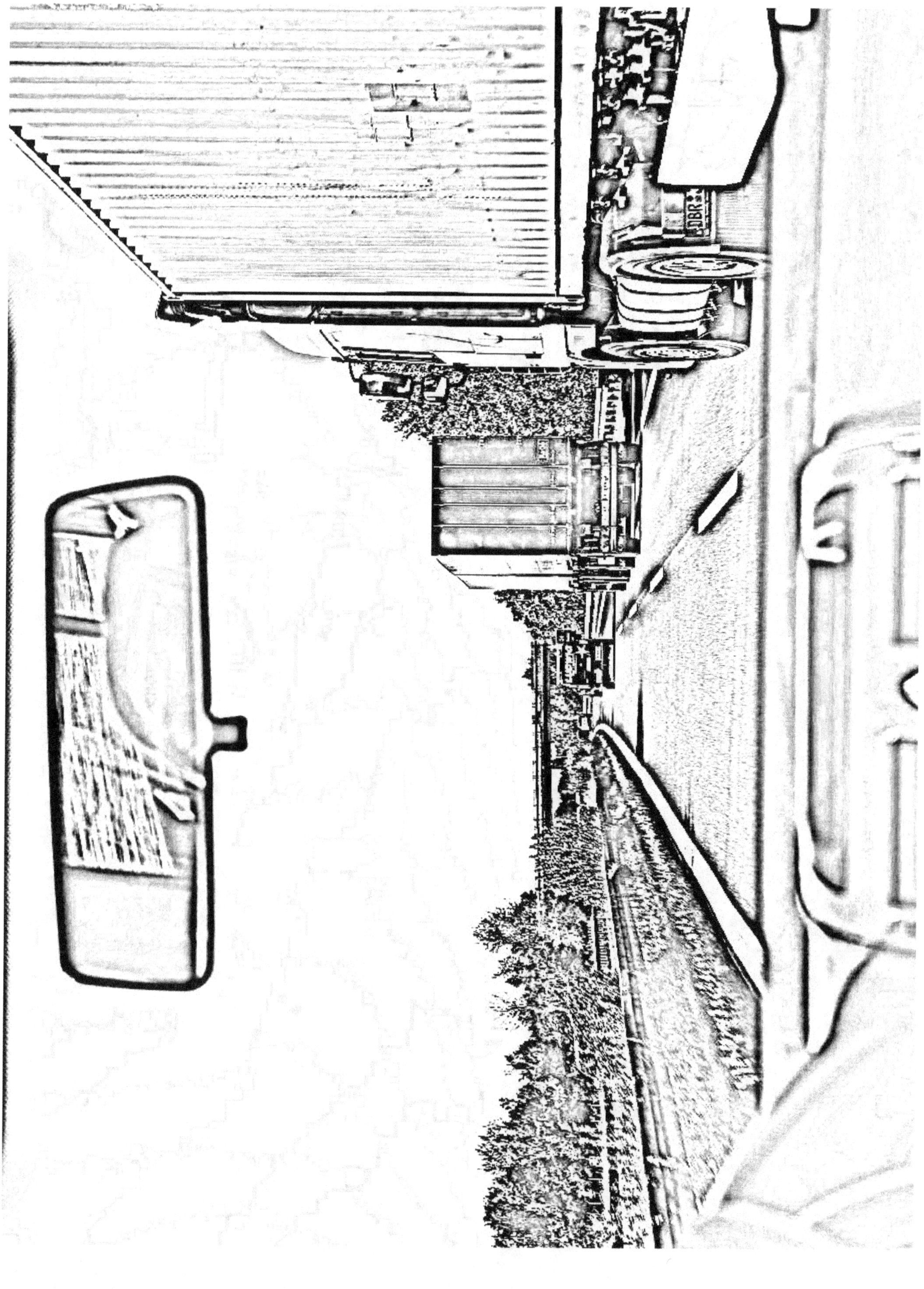

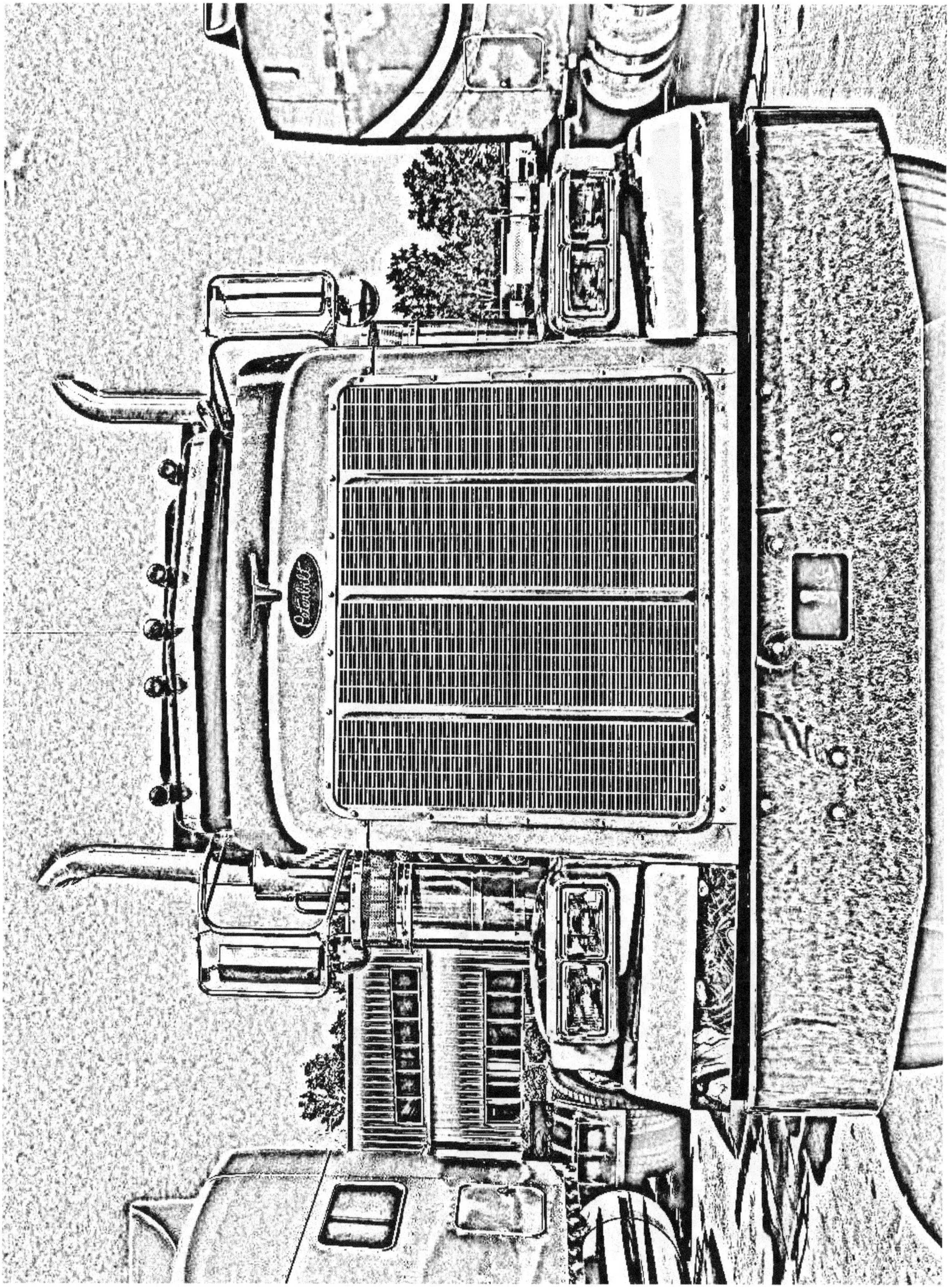

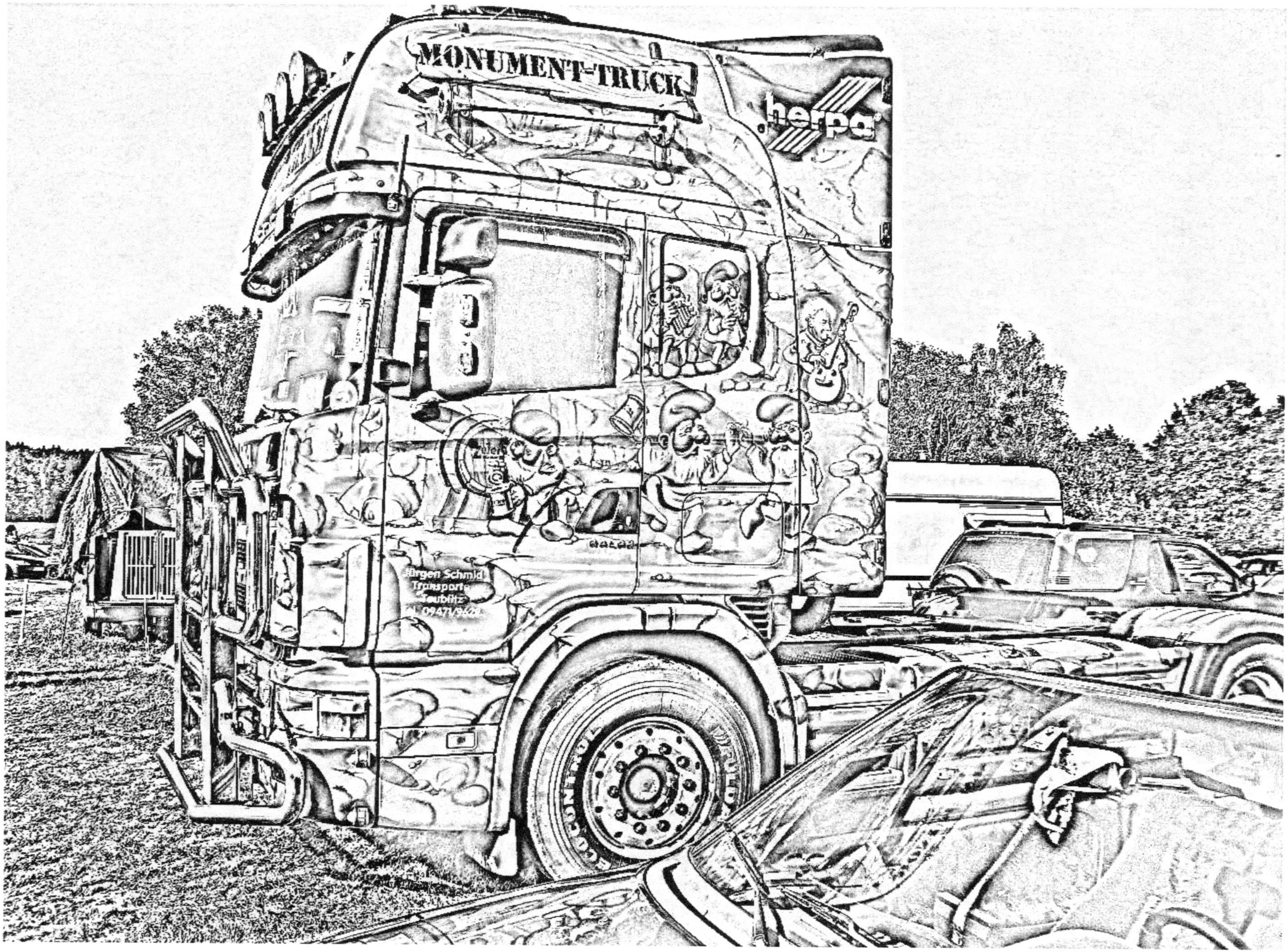
MONUMENT-TRUCK
herpa

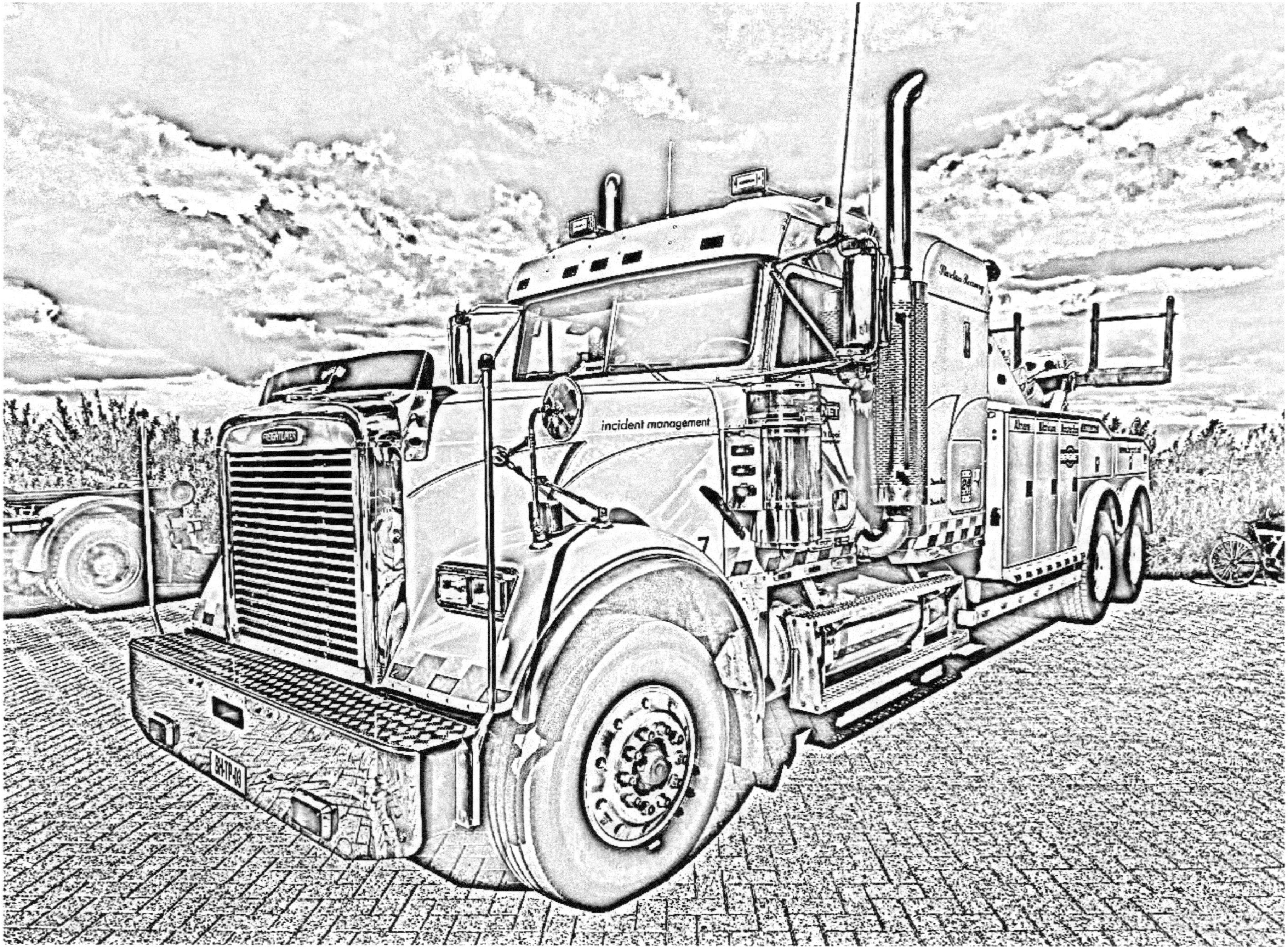
incident management
FREIGHTLINER

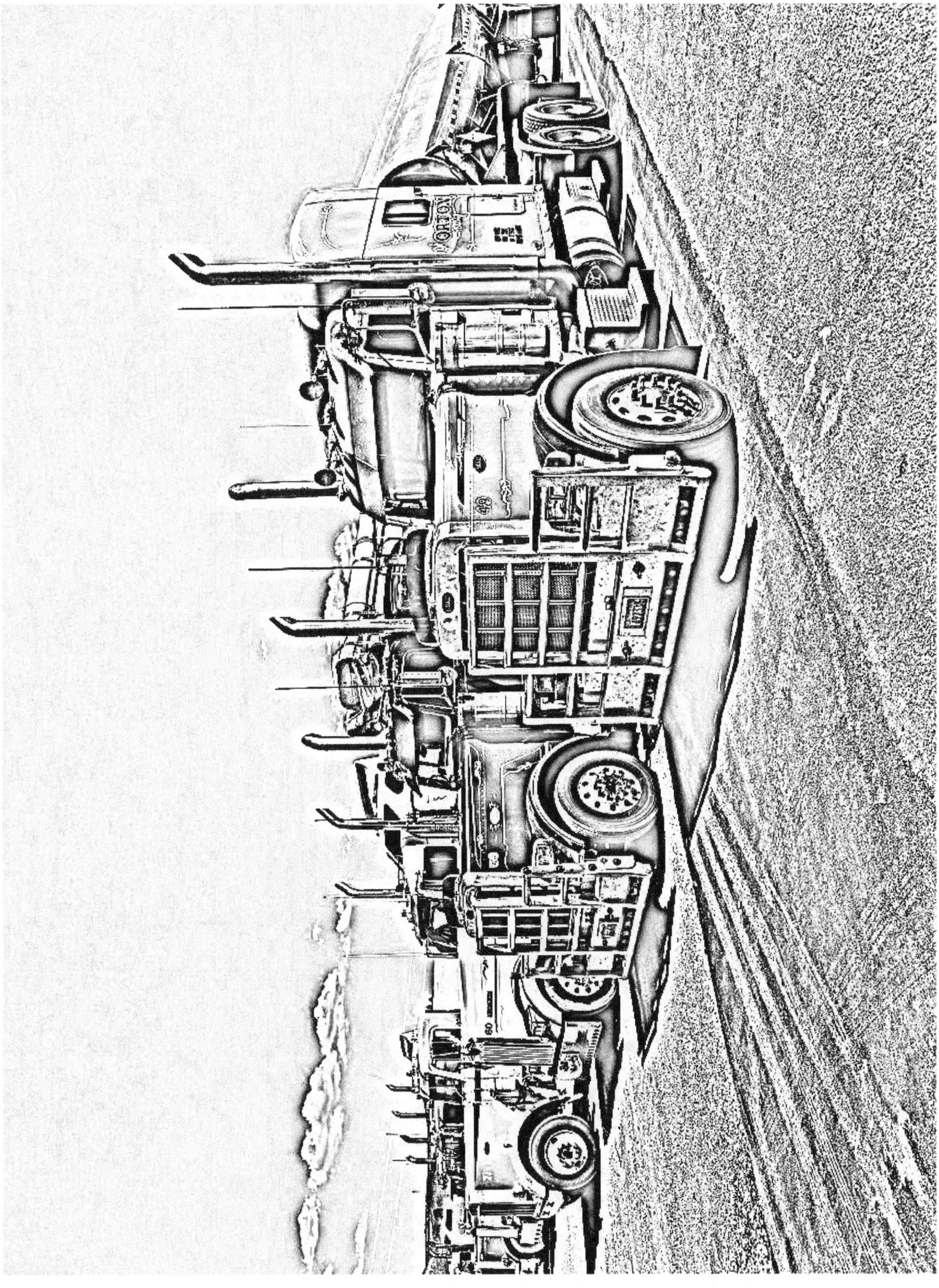

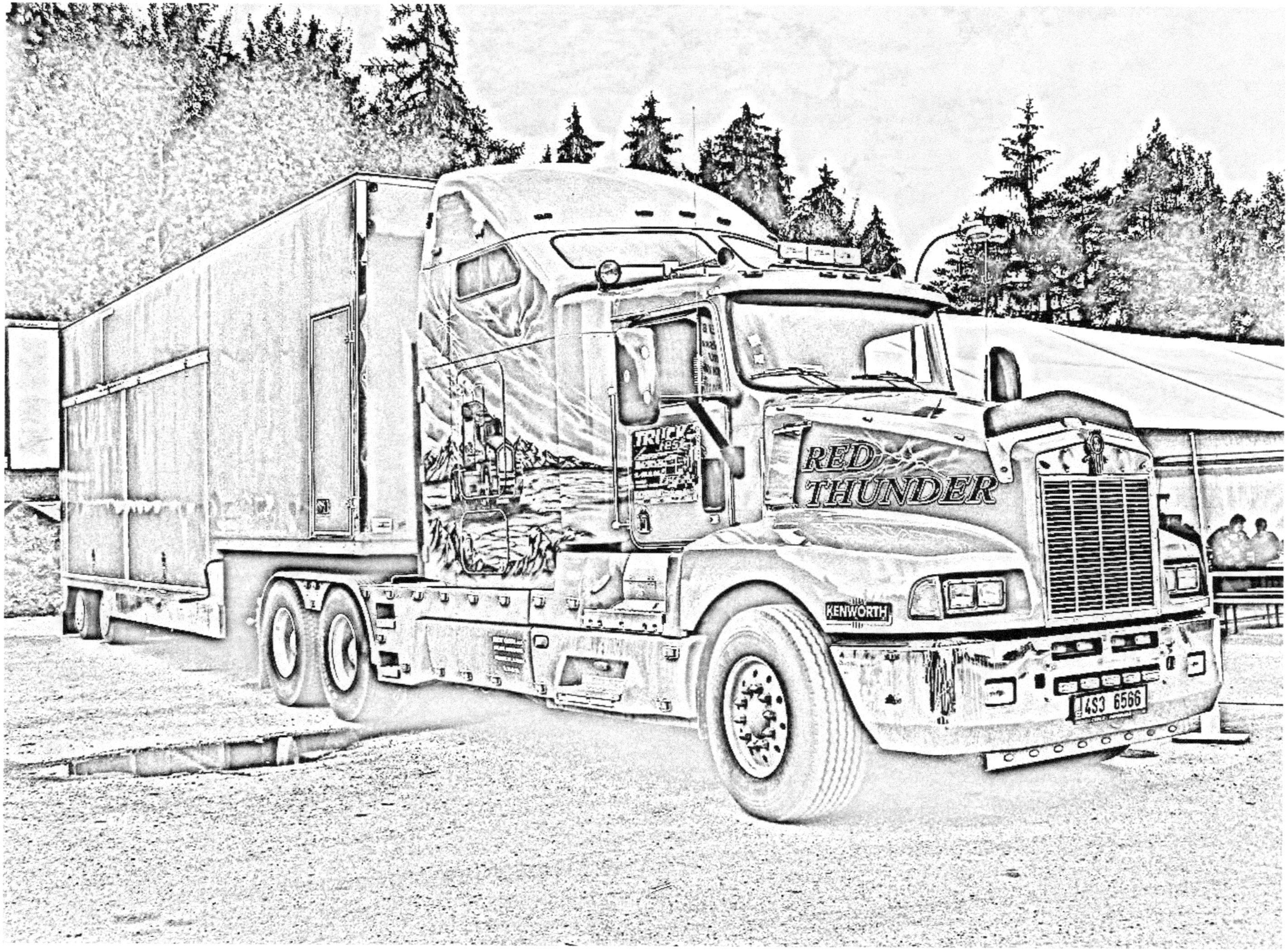
RED THUNDER
KENWORTH
4S3 6566

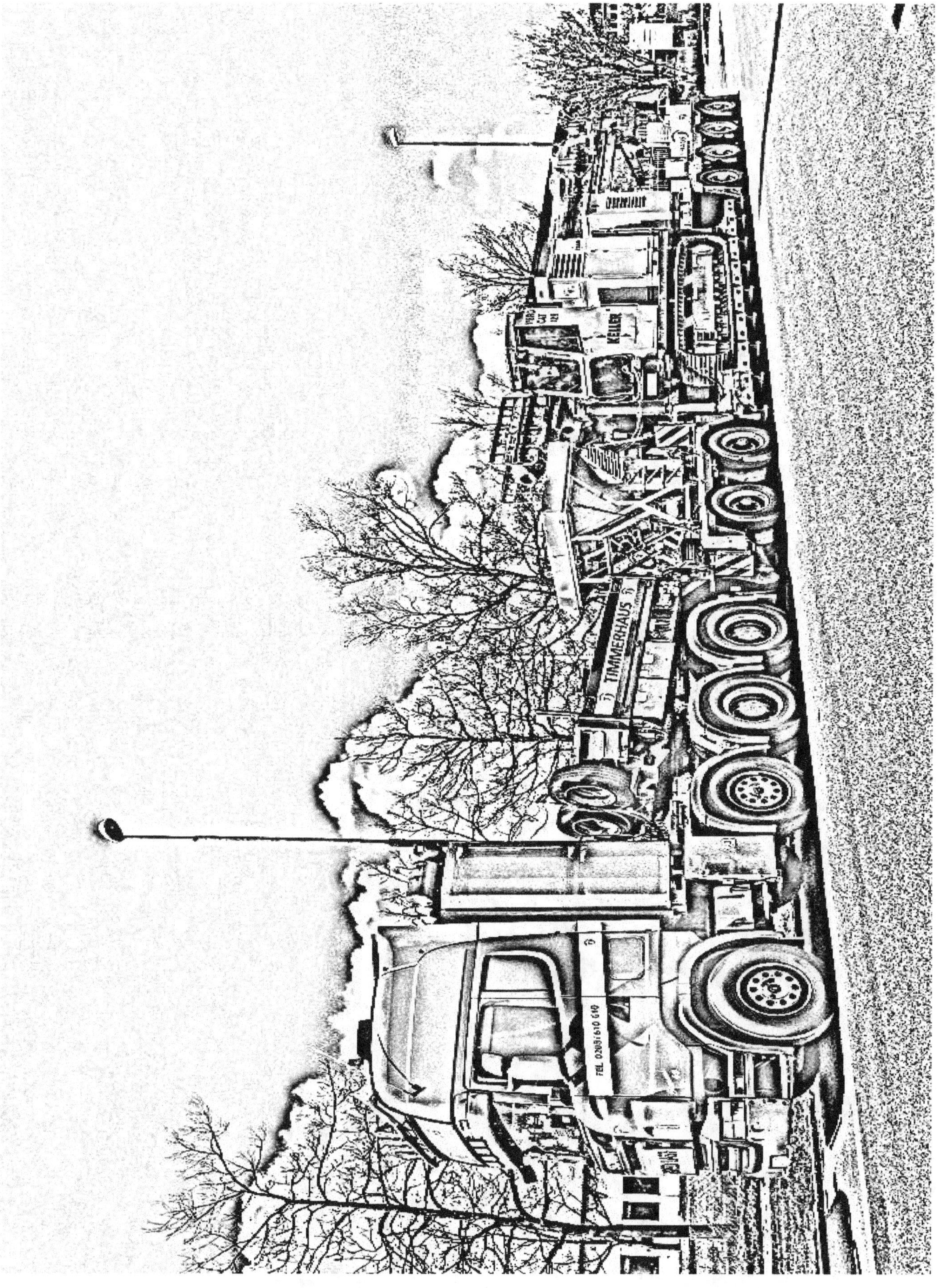
TIMMERHAUS

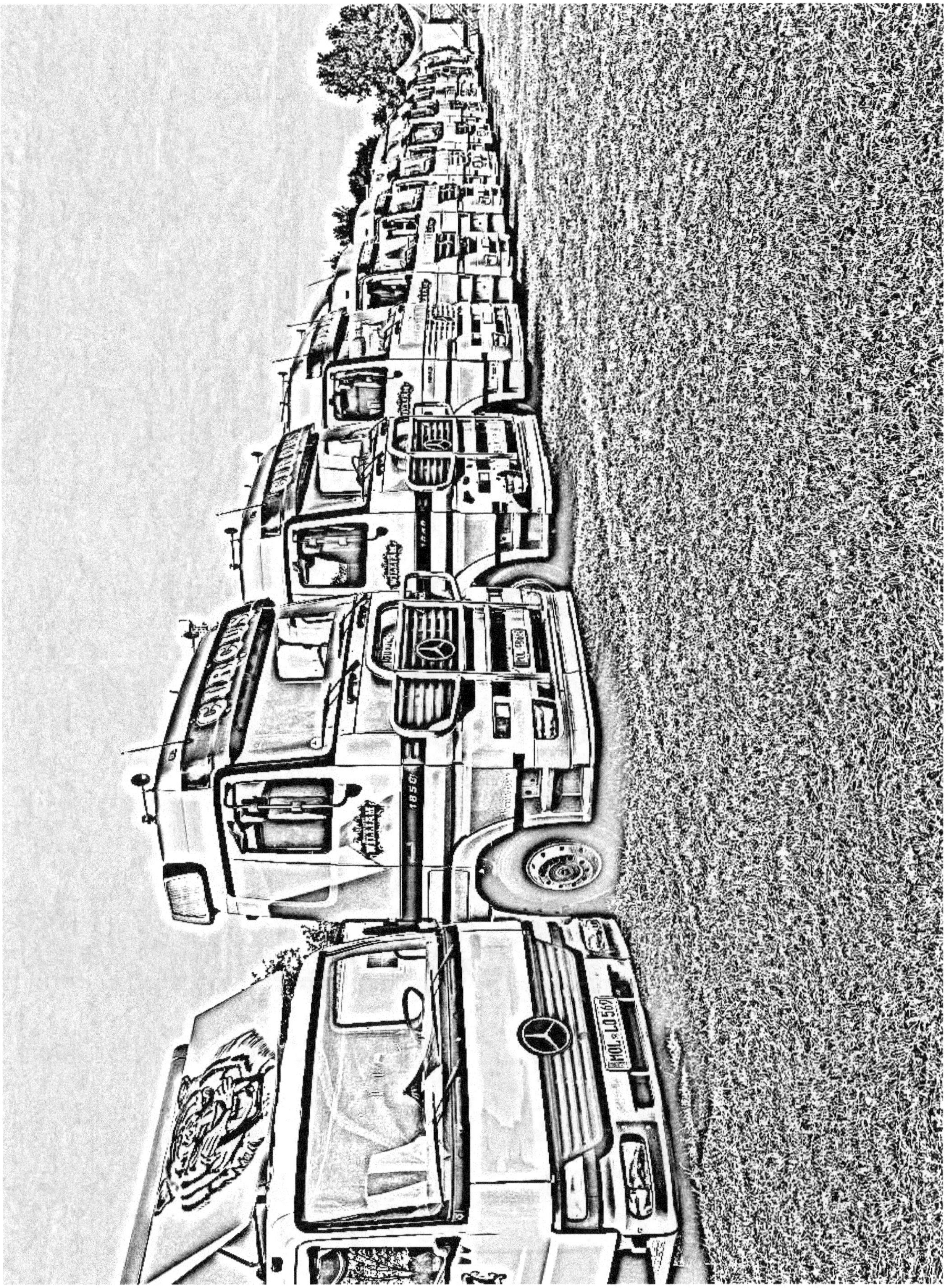

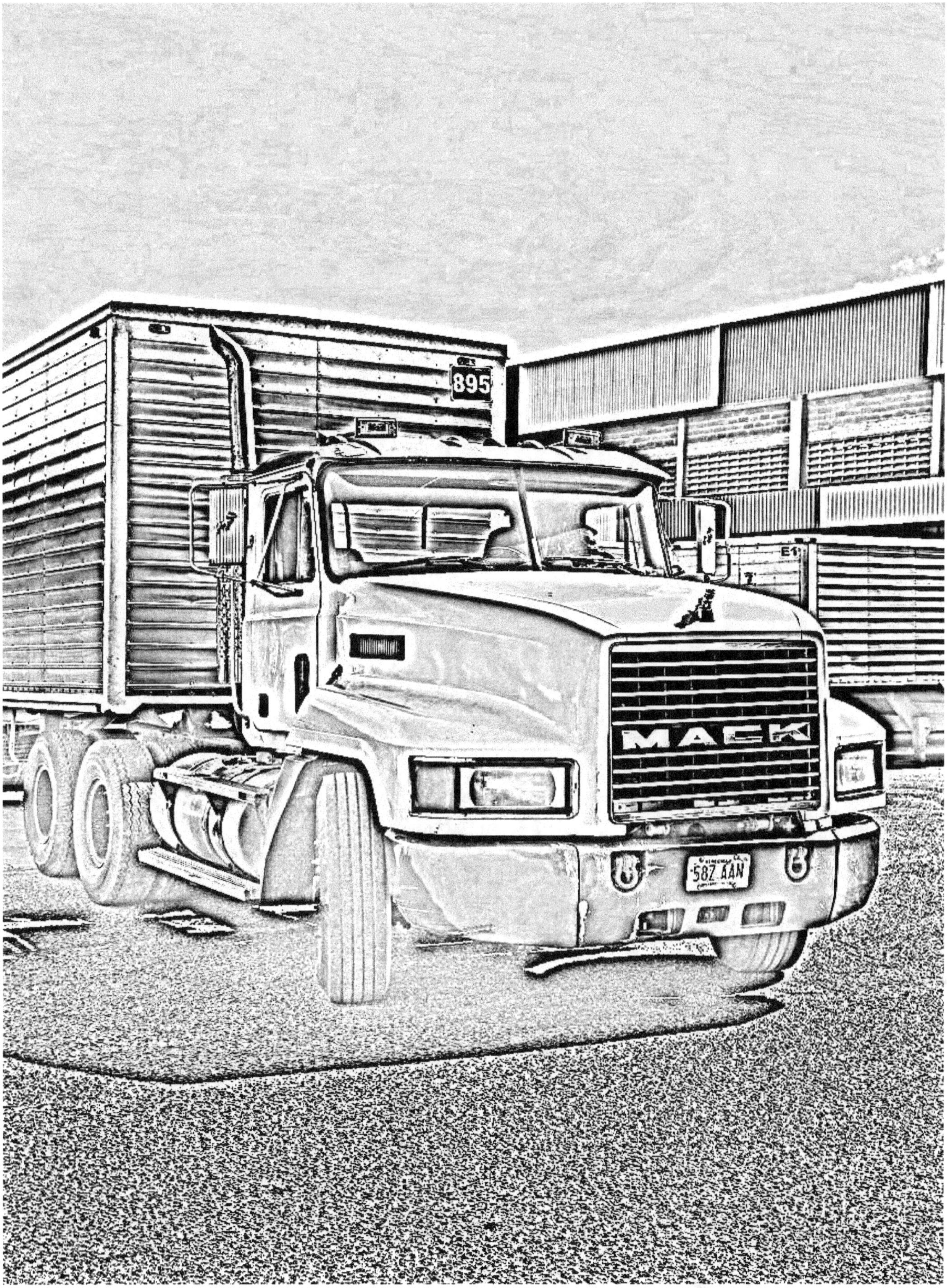
895
MACK
58Z AAN

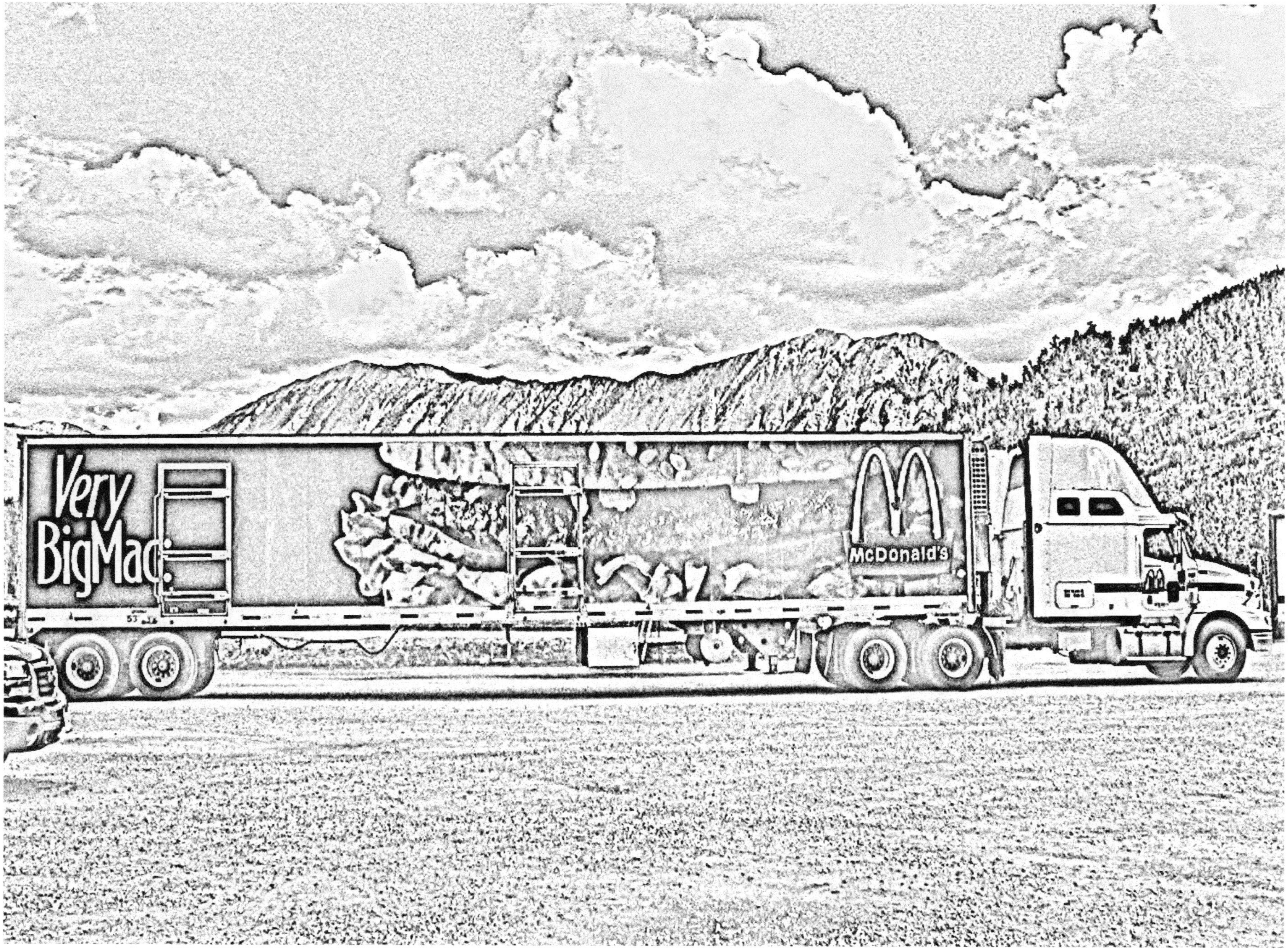
Very
BigMac
McDonald's

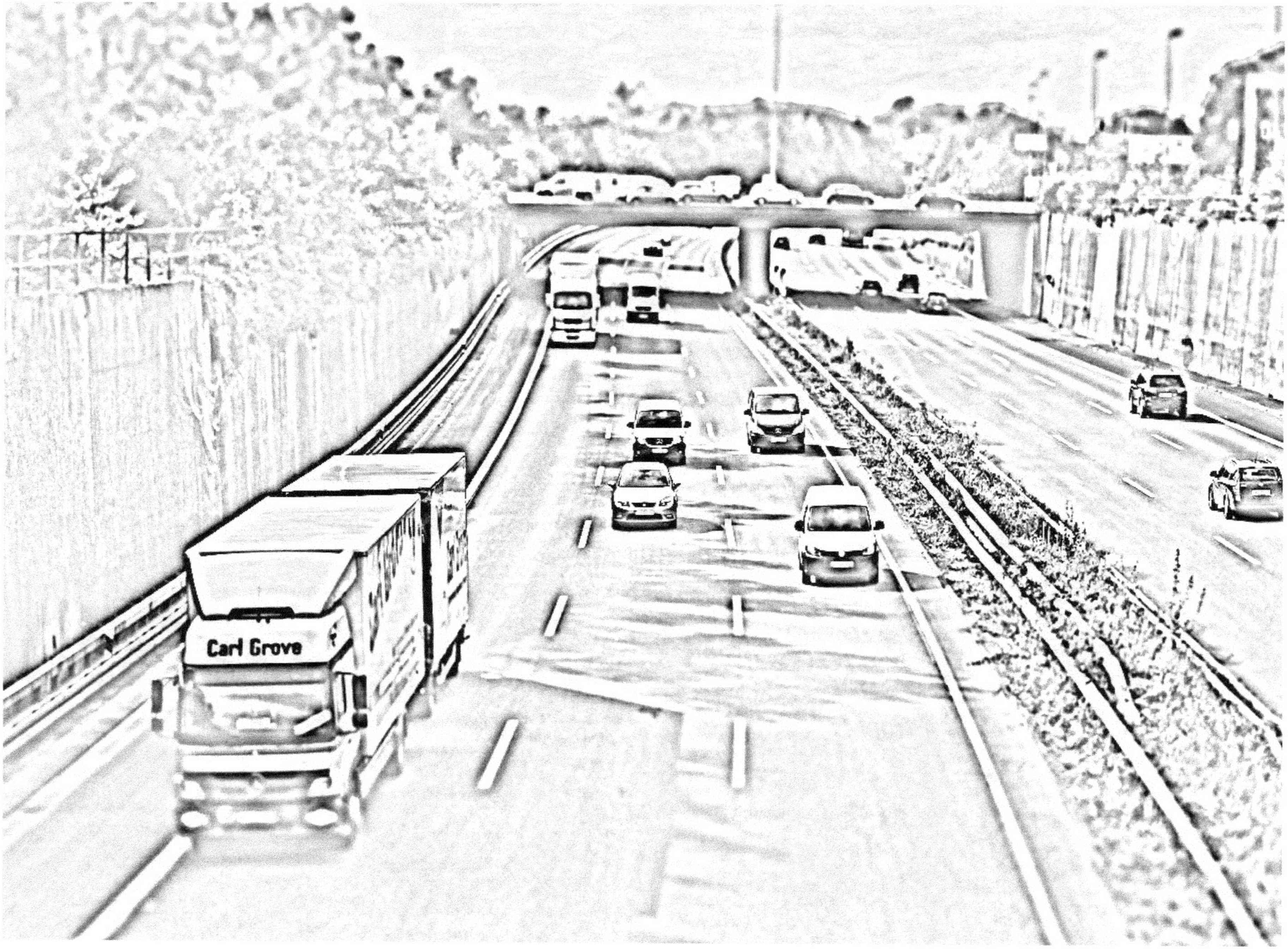
Carl Grove

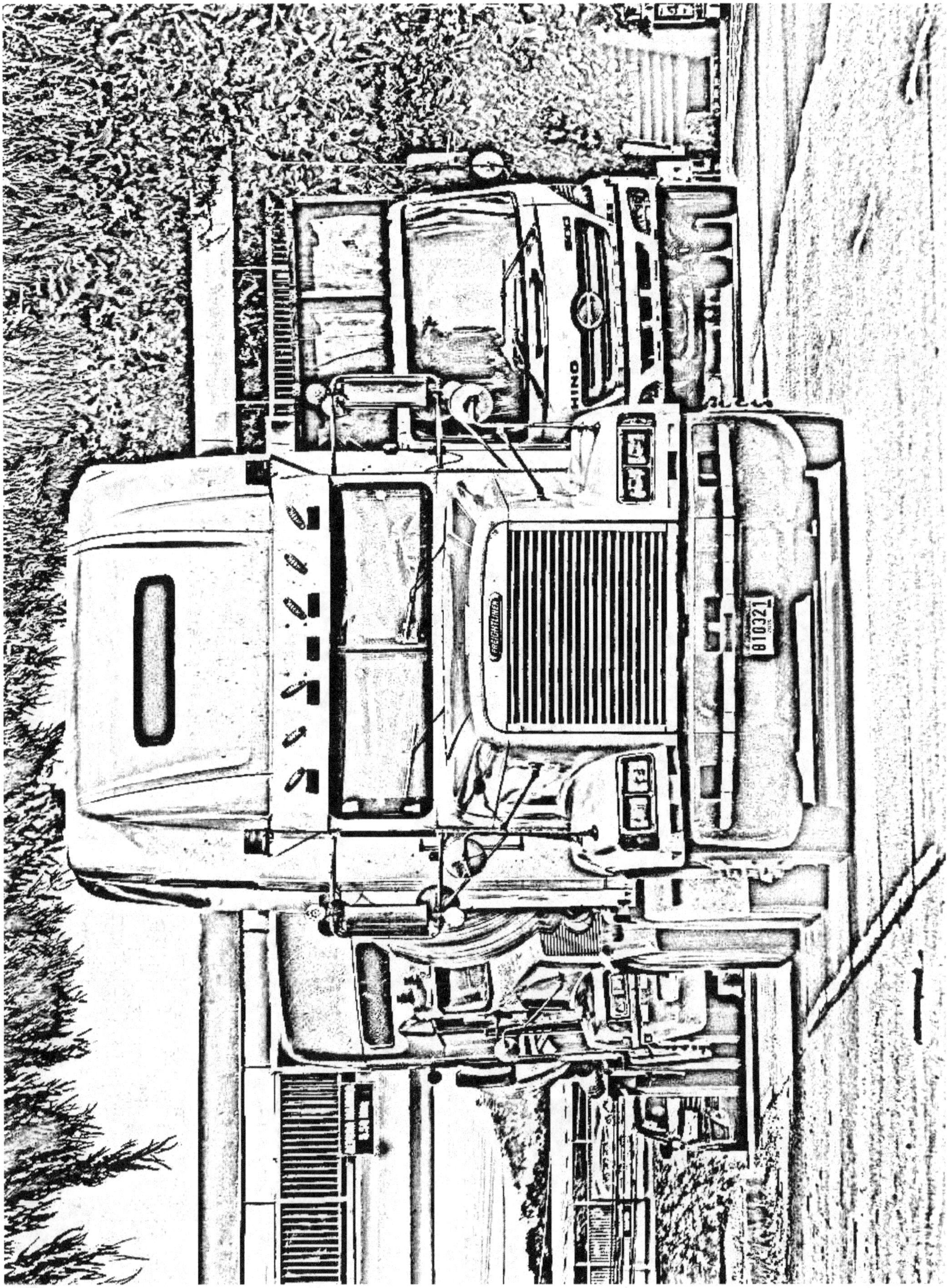
FREIGHTLINER
HINO

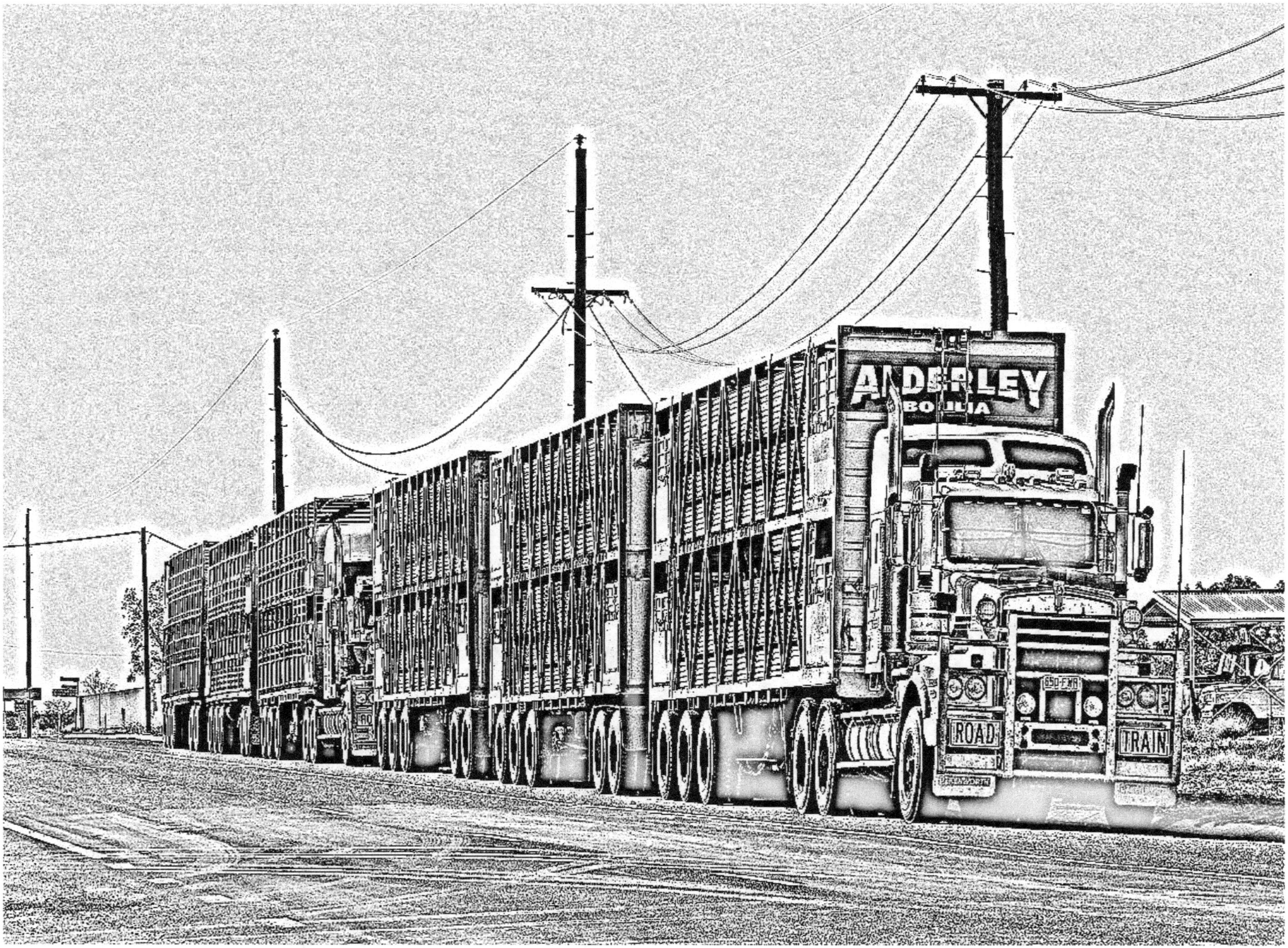
ROAD
TRAIN

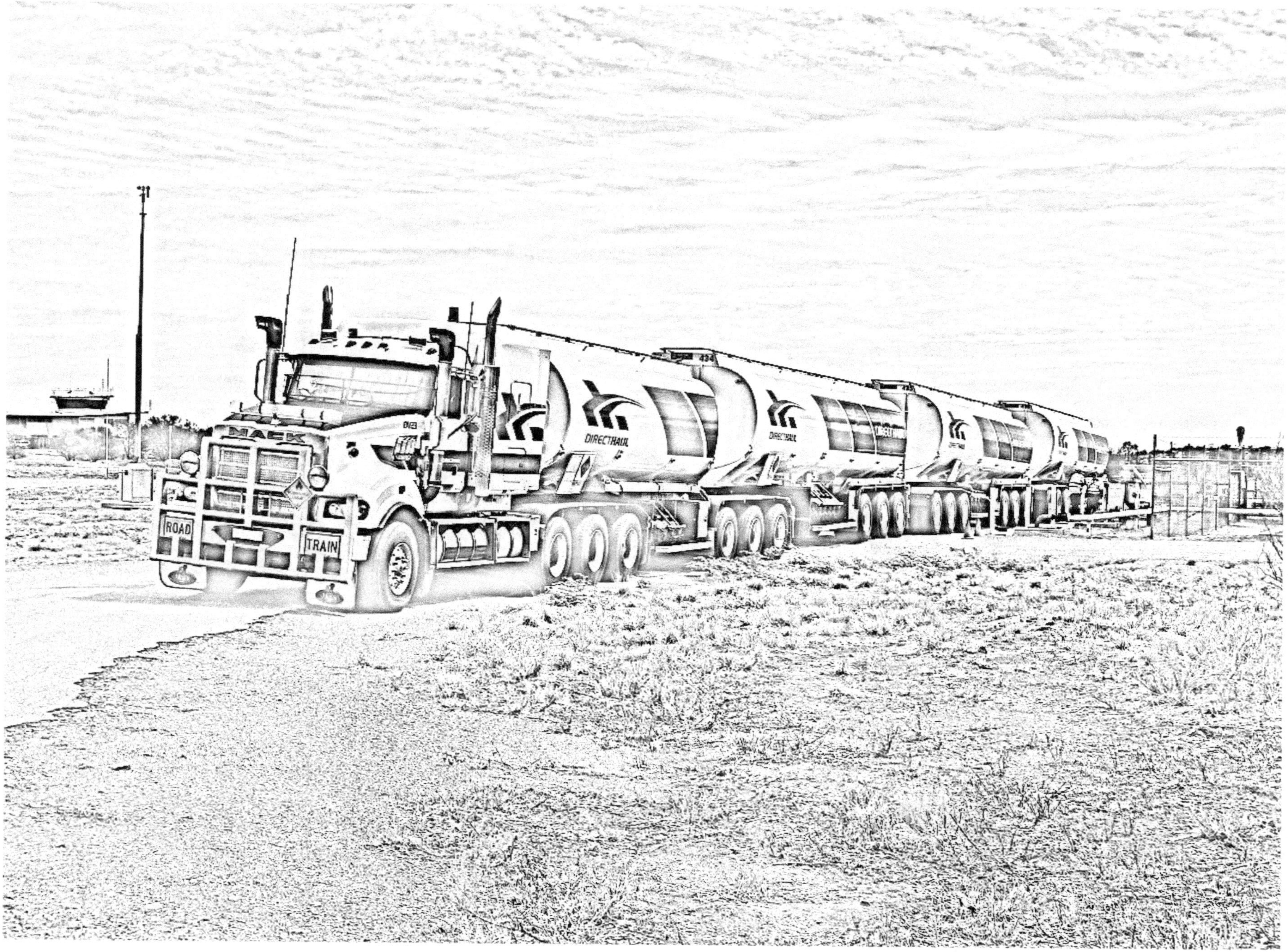

MACK
ROAD
TRAIN
DIRECTHAUL

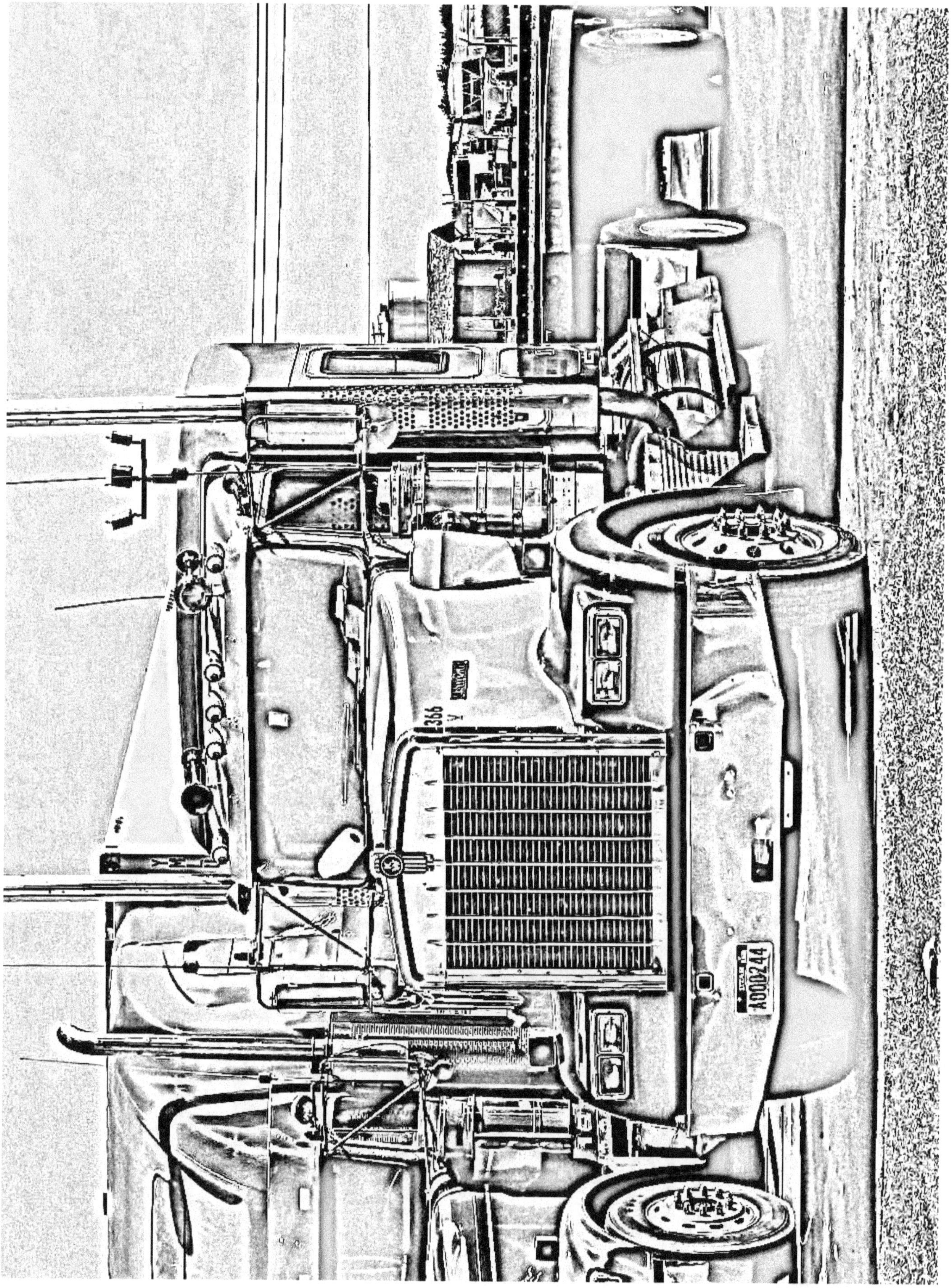

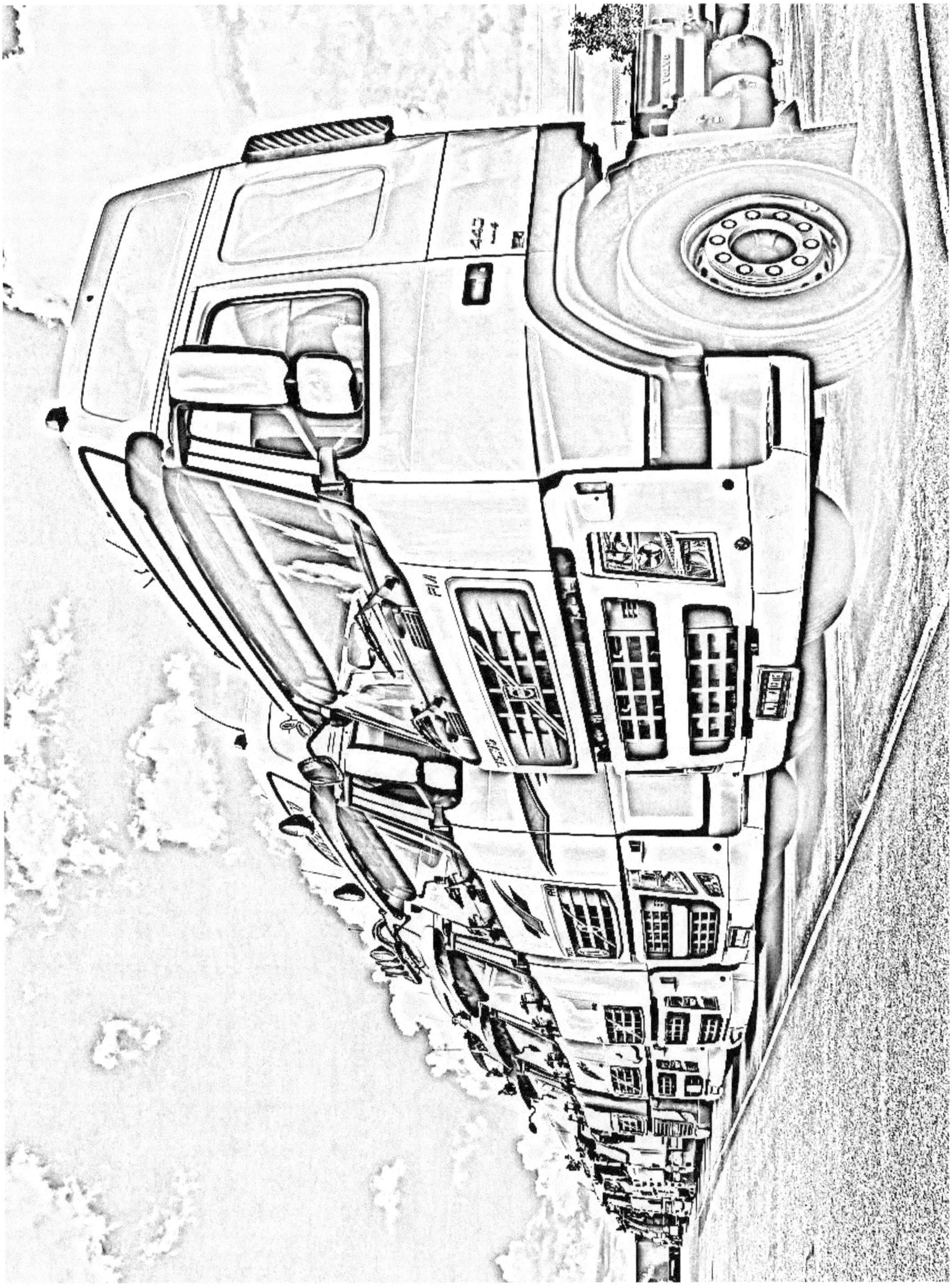

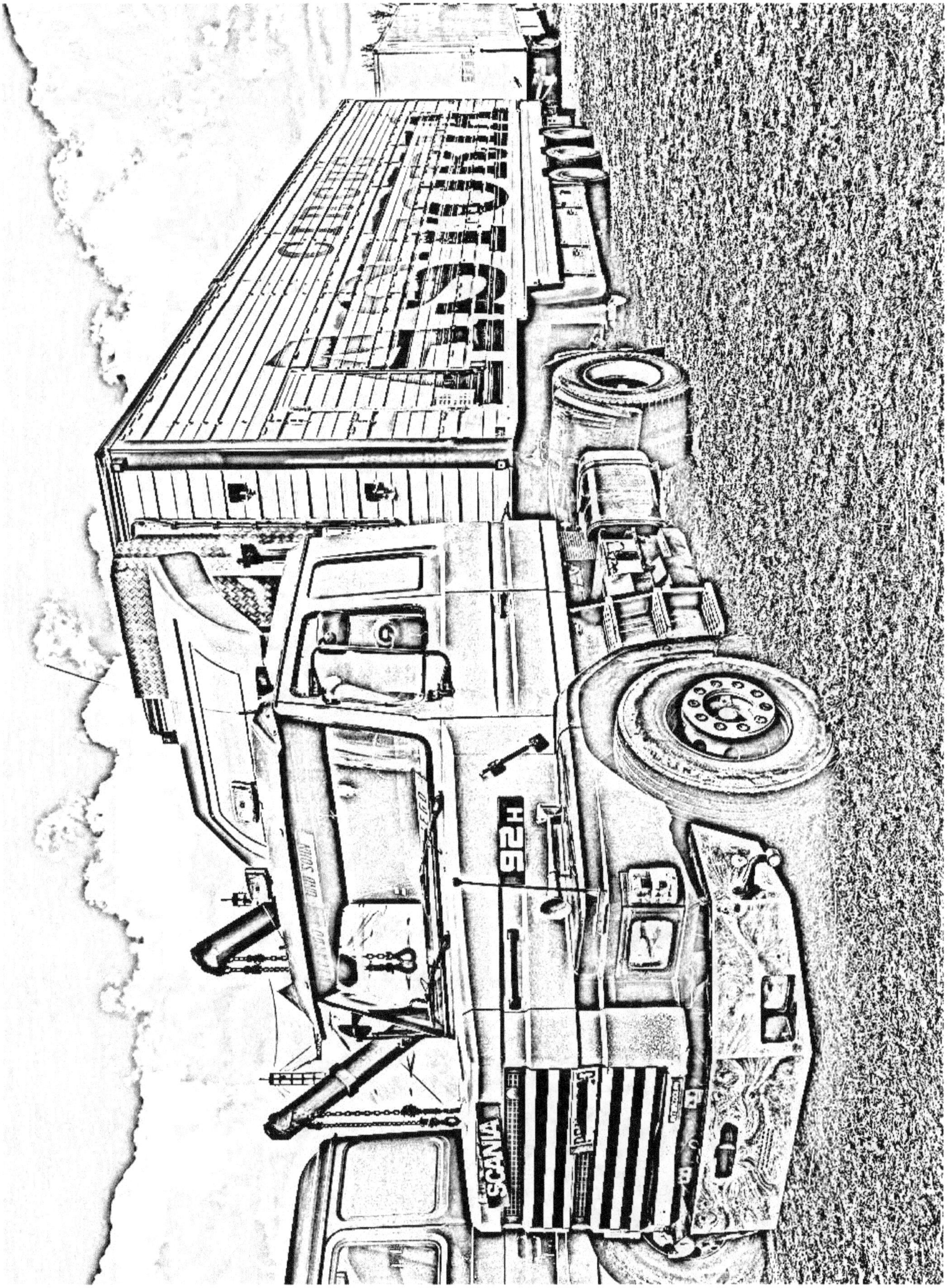
SCANIA
92H

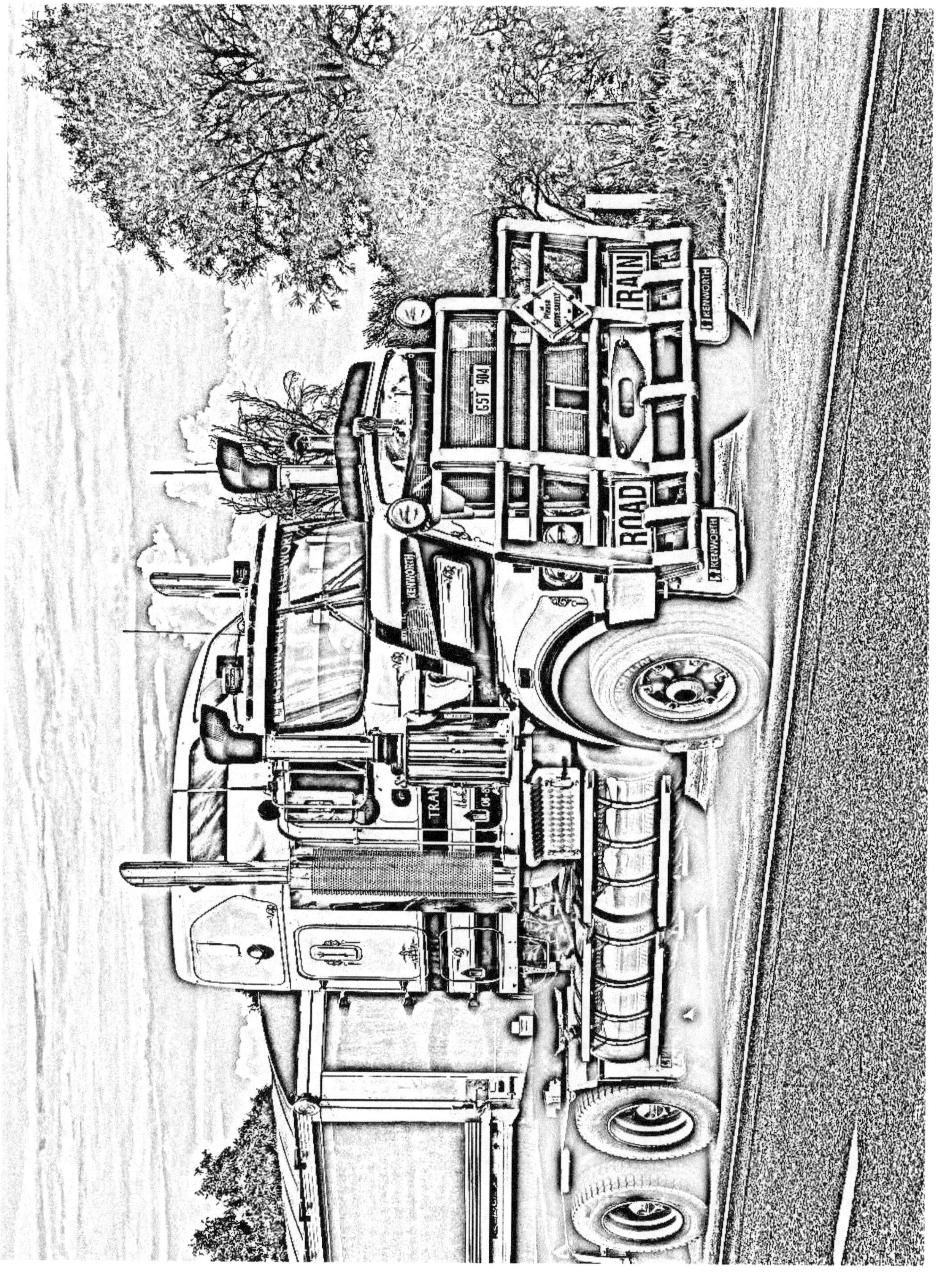
ROAD
TRAIN
KENWORTH
KENWORTH
KENWORTH
GST 904

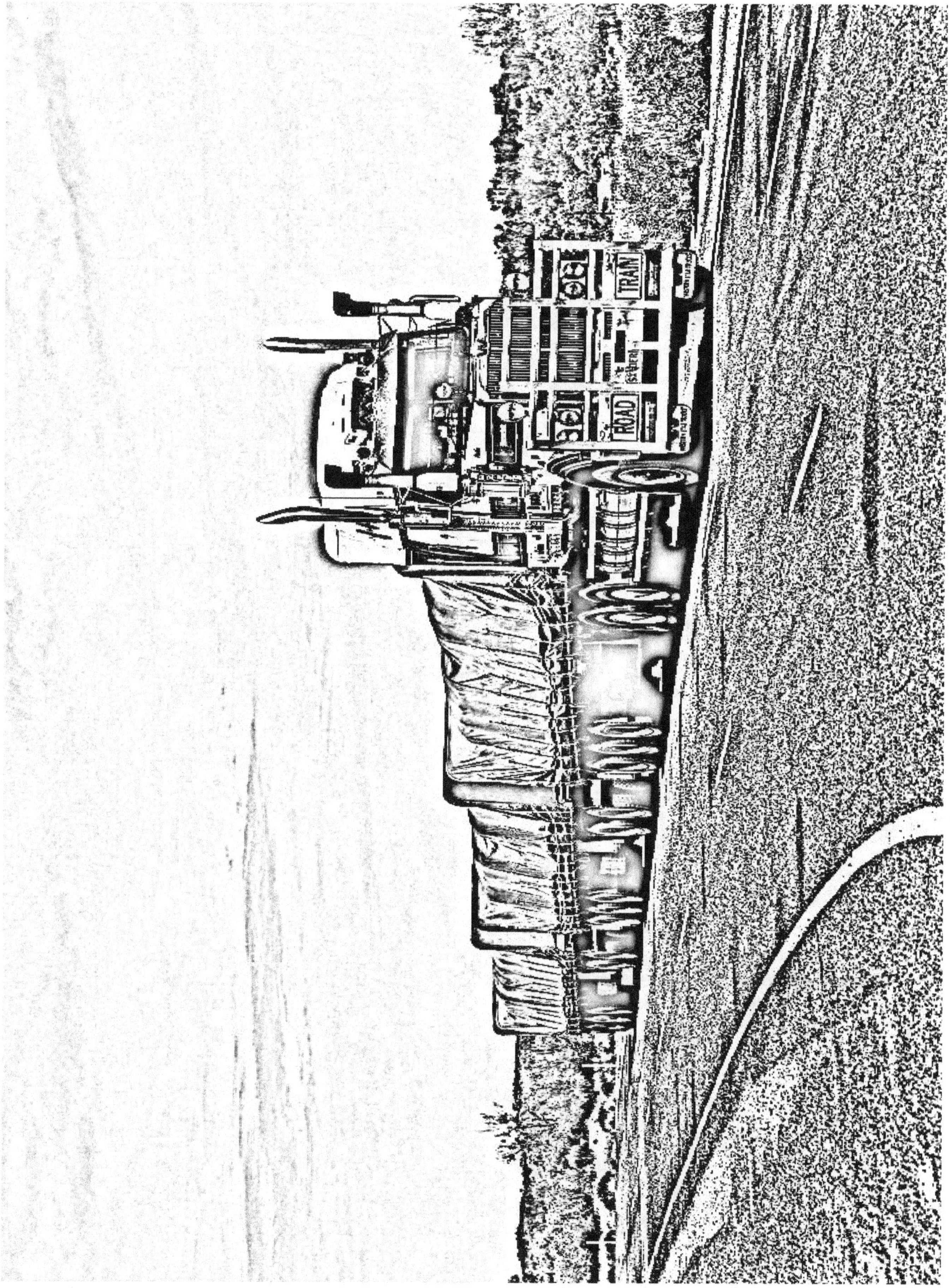
ROAD
TRAIN

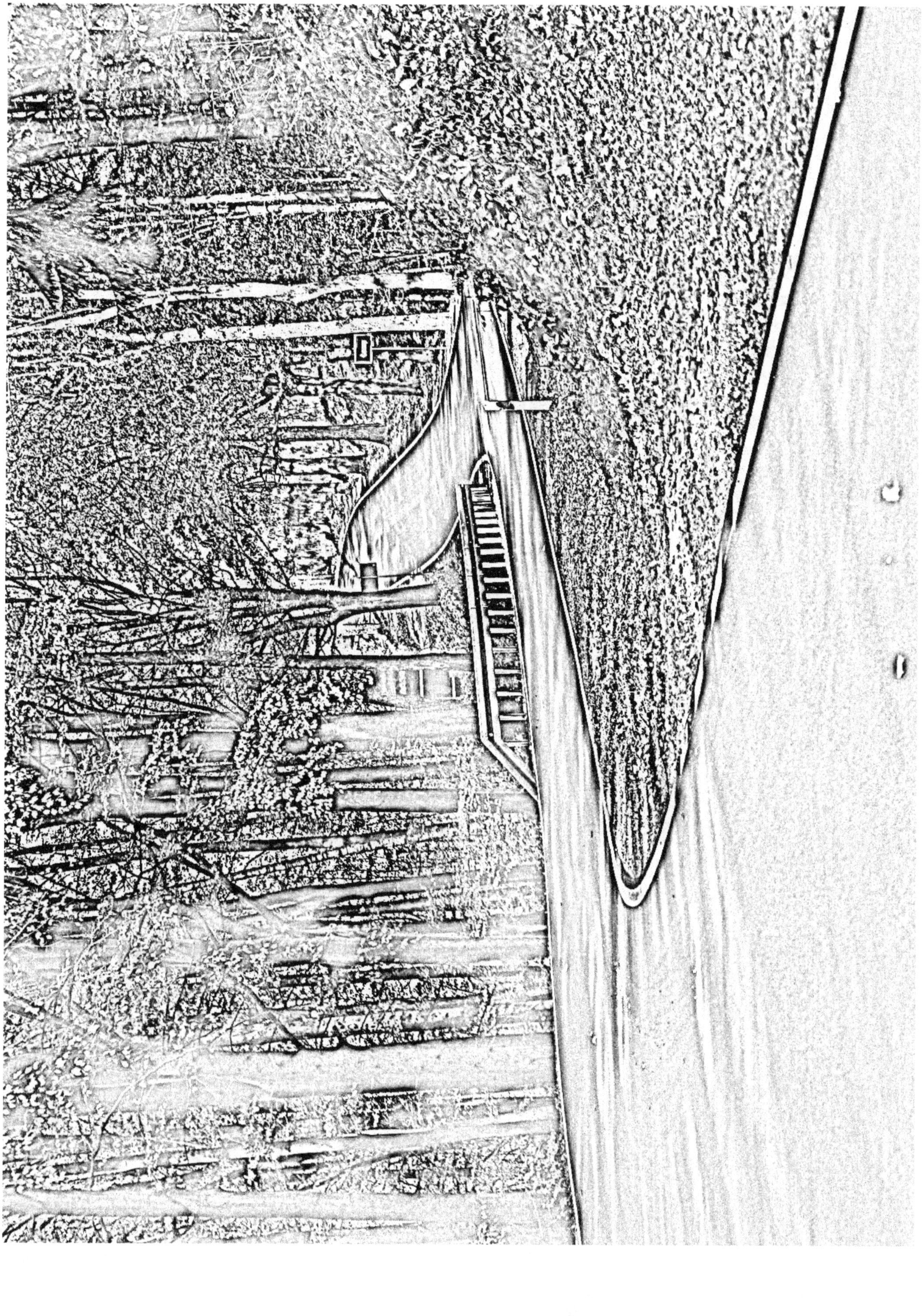

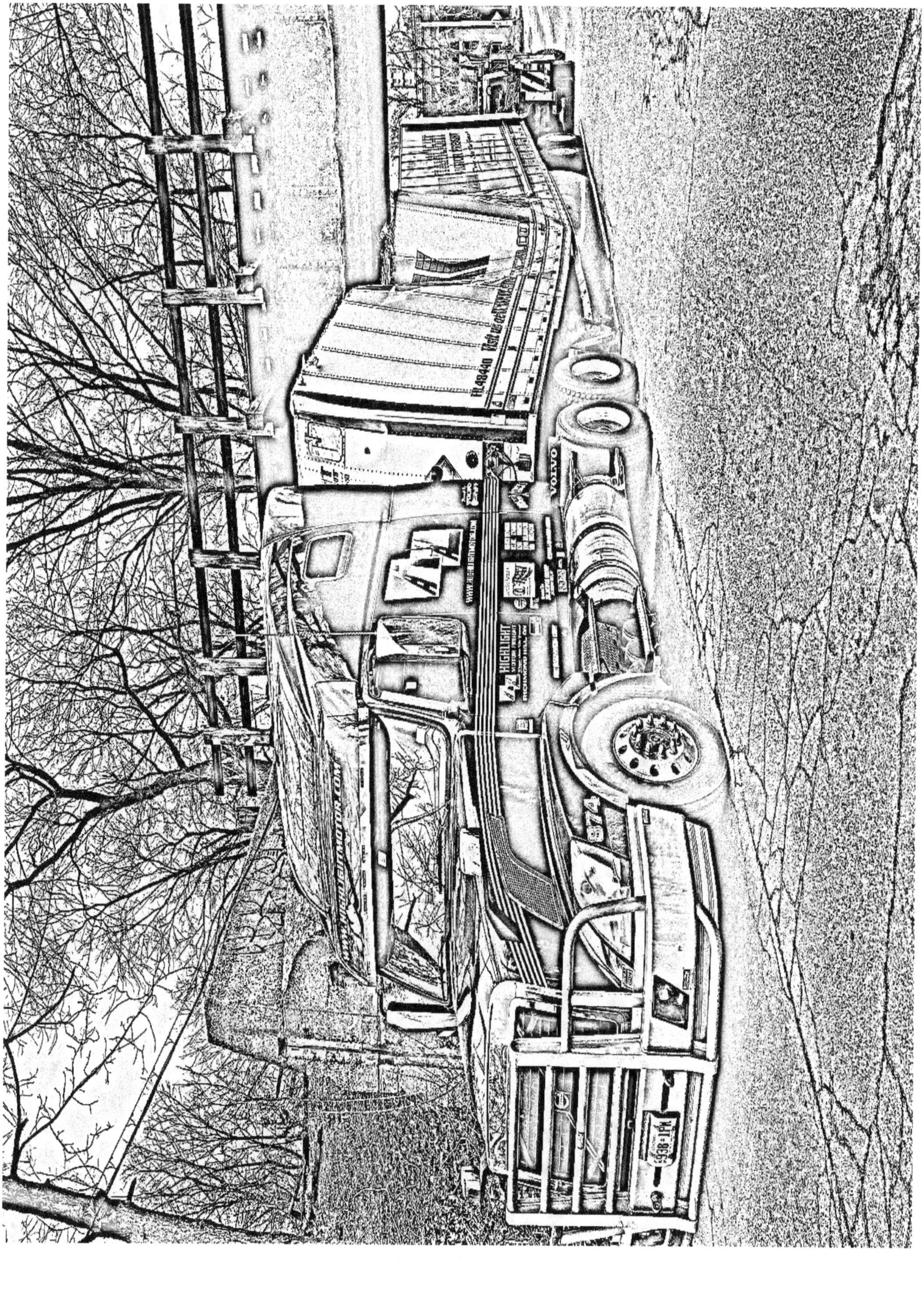
VOLVO
HIGHLIGHT

Thank You!
We hope you enjoyed our book.

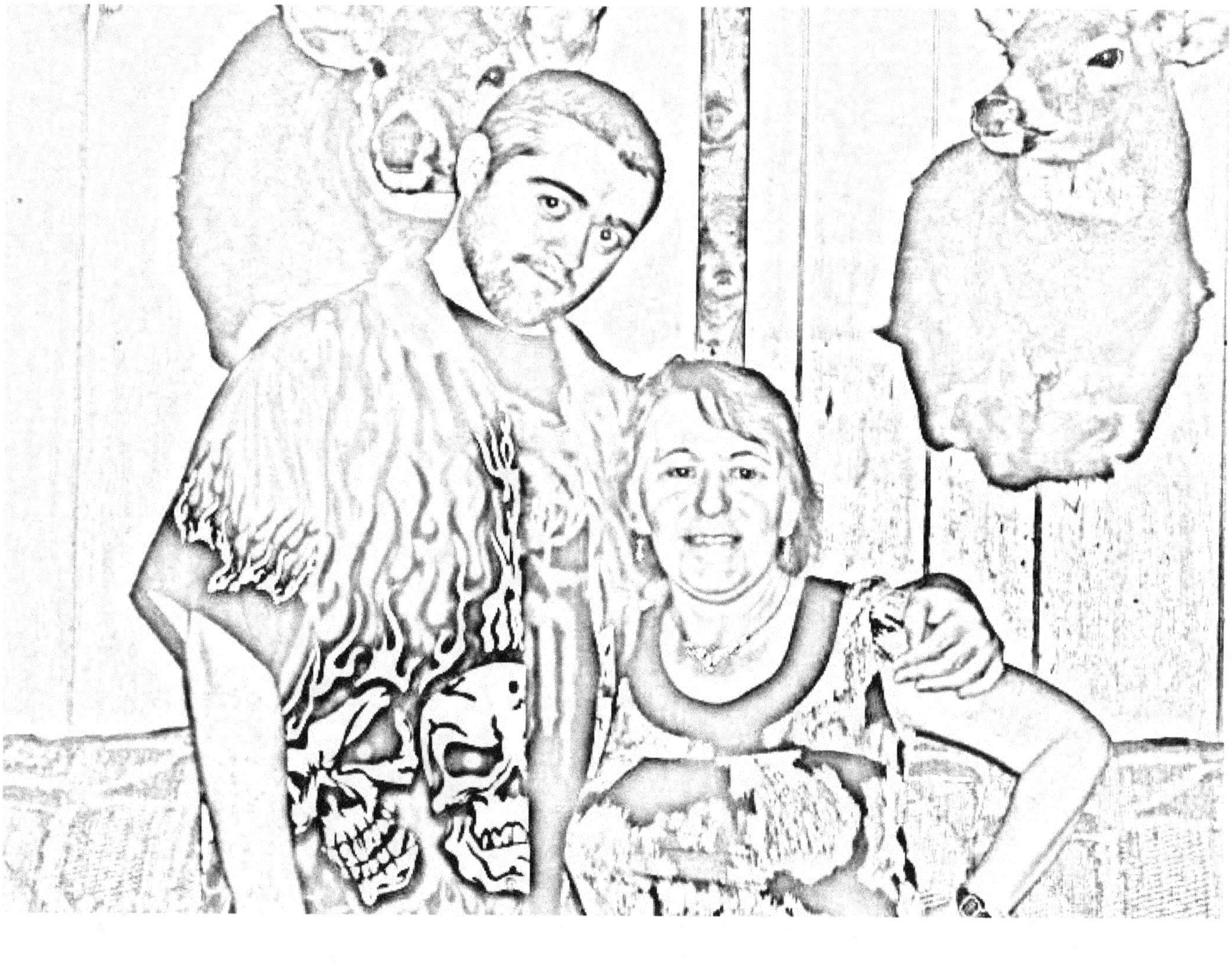

Watch for more color books by ARN Arts LLC.
Visit us at http://arnarts.wixsite.com/books

www.ingramcontent.com/pod-product-compliance
Lightning Source LLC
Chambersburg PA
CBHW081124180526
45170CB00008B/2997
* 9 7 8 1 5 4 0 5 2 9 6 5 7 *